QUESTIONS ON YOUR HEAD

Become The Best Version Of Yourself

Bob Sharon

TABLE OF CONTENT

Question on Your Head" is not meant for those in their early 20's alone, it's for everyone who has faced disappointment and was stuck with the question why on their head instead of asking for ways forward, as well as for those who may have kept up their faith by trusting humans like them instead of believing in what they can do. In the case of this book, we have highlighted in the basic fundamental shift in perspective how important it's to traverse life's uncertainties. The inspiration behind this book comes from recognizing the prevalent tendency to dwell on the question "why" when faced with challenges or uncertainties. Through my experiences and observations, I've come to understand the limitations of constantly seeking reasons or explanations for every situation.

Specifically, Question on Your Head lies in emphasizing the power of focusing on what now rather than getting stuck in the loop of questioning why This shift in mindset is transformative, as it directs every form of energy towards active steps, problem-solving, and personal growth. This book is basically structured to empower you to embrace uncertainty as a catalyst for action and opportunity, rather than a source of confusion or doubt.

By implementing every analyzed point stated here, you, as an independent person, will single-handedly make an adjustment whenever there are problems that some individuals encounter and get struck, creating more problems for themselves while trying to come out of them. Here, I aim to equip you with practical strategies and clear goals to scare through lives, rotate and turns with confidence and clarity. It reviews the actual power of embracing the unknown, finding purpose in challenges, and moving forward with determination.

Majorly, " Question on Your Head" is deeply endeared with food of thought, basically created for personal empowerment, encouraging you to shift your focus from always taking control in every challenge you encounter in life or seeking all-encompassing answers to embracing the present moment and taking reasonable steps towards a fulfilling and purposeful life.

When it comes to life matters, we often find ourselves entangled in threads of the past, weaving circuitous patterns of whys and "what ifs. Yet, amid these complexities, there lies a simple truth waiting to be unraveled the power of focusing not on the questions that bind us to history but on the paths that lead us forward.

Question on Your Head drilled deep into a journey of introspection and empowerment, urging us to release the burdens of yesterday's uncertainties. It challenges the conventional wisdom of seeking explanations and instead advocates for embracing the unknown with courage and clarity.

Go through these pages, and discover the liberating essence of letting go, not just of past events but of the need for constant justification, you will learn that true trust begins within, grounded in a deep understanding of one's capabilities and convictions.

This book is not a strategy to certainty, for life's twists and turns defy such simplistic guides. Instead, it is a companion on your quest for flexibility, reminding you that every challenge is an opportunity to redefine your journey, to ask not why but what now?

As we experience every bit of human relationships, Question on Your Head" illuminates the pitfalls of misplaced trust, urging caution in building pedestals based on past achievements. It encourages a discerning eye, one that sees beyond distinction to the essence of character and integrity.

I also reviewed how you will encounter stories of triumph over doubt, of flexibility in the face of uncertainty, and of the transformative power of shifting focus from the past to the present moment.

Have you observed the lives of those who put their trust in others? Experience should be a better way to enlighten each and every one of us in this case of trust. Imagine waking up in your early twenties only to realize that every person who lived with unwavering trust eventually faced heartbreak and deep humiliation. But it's not too late for you. You can make a significant difference in your own life, avoiding the pitfalls that many faced when they trusted blindly and ended up in regretful situations. They found themselves asking the same haunting question in their late thirties, why did I trust so blindly, and why did I let myself be hurt?

The harsh reality is that by their late twenties, nearly 95% of those who lived with unreserved trust found them grappling with the consequences of their naivety. It's time to stop caring about what others think and focus on your own well-being.

Who cares about the reasons why they never seem to care? Have you ever considered that experiences can be the most impactful teachers? Yet, those who have undergone such experiences often struggle to express their lessons effectively. For some, the side effects linger long after the experience, sometimes even until death claims them.

It's a haunting reality, the weight of unspoken lessons carried by those who couldn't find the words or the courage to share their silence resonate through time, a reminder of the importance of not just experiencing life but also learning from it and passing on those lessons, however difficult they may be.

Perhaps it's not just about the experience itself but also about how we choose to respond to it. Do we let it define us in silence, or do we find the strength to give voice to our journeys, no matter how painful or challenging they may have been?

I have a question to ask?

Who do you trust?

Could you have trusted your parents? Do you have a closest friend whom you have trusted?

Who do you love most?

Does the person worth your trust?

Who else worth your trust? No body, are you sure you are not making a mistake?

Listen to yourself slightly and hear what your answer could be.

You trusted right? Yes.

You may have trusted someone not by mistake, you deliberately did it.

See how you built your first trust with your mom is that a lie?

Does the trust truly worth it in the end? Despite showing immense love to your father, did it end in praise? Perhaps you're yet to encounter the harsh reality of placing trust in others, but let me caution you that trusting people can often lead to disappointment. Those who've trusted blindly before seldom find true happiness in the end.

The real question emerges when your mother receives her first divorce letter. How did you emotionally react? Was the trust you had in both your parents still intact? Even if she never received such a letter in her life, did the loss of the most beloved person in your life shatter your trust, or did it remain resilient in your heart?

Think back to someone who made grand promises to support your dreams and career. Did they fulfill their promises as expected? What was it that made you vow never to trust anyone again?

Now, reflect on the factor that shattered the trust you once held with someone, leading you to believe that it could end in disaster.

Is it:

Lying

Selfishness

Unreliability

Negative Gossip

Disrespect, because this are one of those things that always seen at the first stage when trust are built.

This are the most common one people encounter on their everyday life but those are not the ones that hurt the most.

There are mini ones that people hardly notice but kills trust more than those ones that they encountered in their day to day life.

Have you ever had the opportunity to ask the dead why?

I mean why they died without fulfilling the promises they made?

What could be the answer that you may have received? If there is this say, that death is inevitable.

Then loved ones whom you may have lost to death will they tell you the reason for their early departure and why they left even when you needed them most?

Sorry, this is still part of the disappointment one can witness if he trusts fellow man more than he trusted himself.

You may have actually had a dream like every other person does yes! But, then what was your offense where did you get it wrong.

Are you happy? You need to smile, not because you are happy but self- love is the real deal.

I wish I could tell you this full story but time may probably not permit.

The reason why I have to say a bit of it is that it was all about the trust I had with my father and the result was so humiliating and frustrating at the end, but then I never know whether to say that the worst mistake I made was to build a strong trust with my father to the extent that even my career was also built in his already acquired success.

Did you hear me say a dream built on my father's already achieved success?

Yes I did, have you ever trusted so much?

If yes, listen and hear me well may it not get to the extent of building your career trusting that with your father, mother or a close relative, if you have ever done that I must tell you that it may be the major reason why you will not achieve it as a dream.

There are lots of tiny factor that ruined the entire trust I built with my father at my early 20s.

Maybe you have as well trusted someone there in your mind, it's normal to do so but with the experience I have had at my 20s, I had to draw the conclusion that life is not fair, As a result there are no tangible reason to trust anyone, not even yourself, because there are some crazy things you have gotten yourself into but you never believed that you did that with your normal senses.

A written note to you, the note is to remind you how crazy it could be to give someone 50% of trust. It may not be necessary that the person wants to betray you initially. For instance, if you had a friend whom you have shared lots of memory with and probably he had an emergency that required some kind of funding to sort it out or there about and pleaded for your assistance, then based on the level of trust you had with him, you decided to assist.

You considered the fact that he was a very good friend of yours and decided to help, but the friend couldn't meet up with you at the actual time you both agreed that he would pay back.

First of all, the trust you had in him will start diminishing at some point. All you will say is why?

But you never did bad thing to help, it's just that you helped out of trust and the whole thing turned out to bring out the true color of someone you trusted most.

What do you stand to learn from this? Even if you trust a friend, there are some things that, when you dream of doing them with a friend or even loved ones, end up bringing out the trust you had on the person to the true test or reviewing the trust in ironic ways.

Take a look at the time I trusted my father with the hope of building my career with his already-acquired wealth.

Did I build my dream on someone's already established success, here the question now come who am I and what I am made off, the truth be told, the question left me with huge surprise. I immediately looked back to realize that my suppose (parents) had been my back bone from kindergarten to college. When I was at my early 18s, this was when the truth about what life is all about showed up. The dream I built on the already-achieved success of my parents was shattered why then should I ask why when I know quite well that it's in human nature to DIE.

Who can ever question death? The scientific discoveries have yet to give a clear detail about what death tells about.

I looked at the scientific discovery of death, as it can be described as the permanent halt of all biological processes necessary for sustaining an organism. For organisms possessing a brain, death may also signify the irreversible cessation of activity throughout the entire brain, encompassing the brainstem. Then, after which, the question now was what's the meaning of life? If the true definition of death is what brought the human race to an end on earth, then the dream which was built on their already-achieved success brought tears and left me with the question, why!

Then who cares if the dreams letter came through after the dismay of my spouse, since my father is lifeless and can't participate in any life activities to pursue the dreams.

Then is the world not a wicked one since nature has it this way, if you had dream placed on the shoulder of people's success that may lead to terrible nightmare, why?

The question may seem simple but quite deep because it do come naturally when, at times, things seems not to be in a normal state.

If you don't see it that way, then check in your own perspective and tell yourself the truth about the reason for the why, as it may not be far-fetched from what it is meant to be.

They must be a reason to ask why, because even when you are working on your dream at times when you have a challenge, you must ask why. Yeah, it's right, lots of reason to ask why exist naturally but there are some that are meant to be, and if you must ask why, it won't absolutely be of good help to your dream and may also draw you back unaware.

Then, based on the journey of life, why is meant to be in every process, but it's a dual process that is not inevitable?

The reason for your why may not quite be the same reason for my own why, then would you ever believe that anyone cares about the reason for your own why? Everyone is interested to hear about the why behind your success, nothing comes out of the reason for not accomplishing your dream.

Now can i shake the dream built on my presumed already-acquired success or that of other people whom I feel have made it so far in life and believed that without them, my dream won't come true since I now know that their life are no longer promising to achieving those dreams.

You know that in life, many things may occur directly or indirectly, which may actually lead you to ask why.

Why should I be happy telling the story of failure when the success has yet to knock at the door? That's an ugly story that no one is ever ready to listen to. But before then, it's very clear to know that failure is never a crime it's meant to be so. Whenever you are shooting a target and you fail the first time, do not ask why. Asking why may create a setback to your progress.

Nevertheless, it is not a bad idea to keep every record of your life journey, as that is part of why both the successful aspect and failure in all aspects can both motivate.

Who has witnessed only success and never failure in life, and why?

Not even the richest man in the current world can attest to that. Then why are you asking why if that happens on your way, be it in your academics, business, relationship, spiritual life, mental life, or career? However, it may even happen accidentally who cares if it occurs in your life as it is part of the life journey in which everyone stands a chance to witness regardless of the field he or she is operating in.

But the reason why failure shouldn't be a hindrance to anyone who really understands what life is meant to be is that it's in human nature to experience failure. Even when you try so much to avoid failure, it can still happen. Let's take a look at it in this form, which aims to understand your ability to recognize your weaknesses and stand up to accept any form of failure that comes your way. This sheds light on the risks you're willing to take, your habits, and your perspectives on success and failure.

It's nice to keep Friends says my old friend and college mate Angelina and I sat on a park bench under the warm glow of the setting sun. With her fiery red hair and infectious laughter, we had a glass of coffee I turned to Angelina with a sparkle in her eyes. "You know, Angelina, I've been thinking a lot lately about the importance of having good friends, especially female friends."

Angelina, her serene demeanor reflecting wisdom beyond her years, nodded in agreement. "Absolutely I have come to realize that female friendships are like precious gems, rare and invaluable. They understand us in ways no one else can.

As the conversation was still ongoing, it came to my mind that I had to ask Angelina, if it's truly important to keep friends, how do I go about getting a female friend who will understand that I have a dream to pursue without asking why? Because I have heard lots of stories about how some gold diggers ruin their male friend's careers. Not quite long ago, a very good friend of mine narrated a story to me about how he had his first ever date with a girl whom he admires so much, and the girl insisted they go to an expensive place, where she ordered a $25 appetizer, a $45 steak, and a $15 drink.

She wouldn't put her phone down and kept taking calls and answering texts.

After which, he was asking himself, Could this be what it takes to have a female friend? This is not giving, I must share with other friends who are more advanced in terms of relationships to seek advice on whether I should continue in this way or else I won't achieve my dream after narrating the whole story of my friend Angelina, telling her the experience my friend had on his first date.

And here was her response to the story, it makes perfect sense to be worried about making real friends those who genuinely support your goals and don't have any ulterior motives. It's understandable to be cautious, particularly in a society where transactional relationships appear to be the norm. But it's vital to keep in mind that not every connection is built on reciprocity. There are many people in the world who respect genuine relationships and who will help you out without asking anything in return. Have faith that genuine connections can be found, and don't be afraid to be open to new relationships. Friendships that support and encourage you are something you deserve, and they are just waiting to be found.

Now she narrated again that they are lots of factors that are needed when it comes to making and keeping friends. Obviously, she hummed and said do you really wish to know?

In a cold voice, I said yes so interested all ears! As a good friend of mine, you first need to value yourself more than anything else before you can think of any other friend.

Now tell me, she said, what do you like most about your life? I lifted my face up and said to her, I do love self-respect, self-worth, and mental and emotional health.

Wow! That is exactly why I must introduce to you those things that are important when it comes to relationships and how you can maintain a healthy relationship without wasting much of your time with gold diggers. As a girl, I know what most girls cherish, which sometimes can ruin their male friends' careers. This is already in a story you recently narrated. But before I tell you that, understand that there are lots of girls out there whose motives are not always to ruin their friends' careers. It's left for you to discover that yourself.

So, for you to have a good and healthy relationship, those things you mentioned earlier that you cherish about yourself are always important to maintain self-respect, self-worth, mental, and emotional health. to maintain that, you have to start on the first date to build them.

Now, how do I build them? That's a very nice question to entertain from you. You have to set some boundaries that will help you regulate every aspect of your life. You wouldn't want your female friends, not only females but all other friends, including myself, to be exempted. As per that, you all have time to say no when it's needed. That will help you beautify your dream and sustain your self-respect, self-worth, mental, and emotional health.

Very nice, then how do I set the boundaries without getting those friends hurt or making them feel bad?

First of all, do you understand what setting up boundaries is, right? I must tell you that establishing boundaries in a relationship helps to ensure that both sides feel understood and appreciated by defining what behavior is acceptable and undesirable. In the absence of defined limits, miscommunications and disputes may occur, resulting in animosity and harm to the partnership.

By understanding the importance of setting boundaries, I have to now come to give you an answer to your question. But before I do that, I must explain something to you briefly. Lots of people who really understand what it's like to be in a relationship know that there are lots that come with friendship, which includes sacrifices. One of those things that they are to sacrifice, if they really love you, is to listen and understand what you love, things that they also love that they wouldn't love anyone in their life to go against.

So, that's actually when you will listen to the person and as well tell the person the kind of thing you hate people doing to you. Then give the person a listening ear to hear what the person will tell you. From the conversation, you will get to know the kind of person you are dealing with, and then the person will also know the kind of person you are. I hope you are now convinced that there is no harm in being in a relationship what matters is the way you handle it by setting up boundaries that will keep you in a safe line of good relationship. Then now tell me, can you give it a trial?

But I must tell you that if you go according to what I have told you by setting up a boundary, I assure you that you won't have a reason to ask why. Because once you ask yourself why it did happened in this way in a relationship, it means that you didn't set a good boundary. Although there is why that may be welcomed, which is the why of surprise gifts and why of great opportunities that came as a result of your friendship, that will actually be of good aid to your dreams. But I must tell that once you ask yourself why when you might have been hurt and it affected your self-respect, self-worth, mental, and emotional health, it means you didn't set up a good boundary, and you have to call your partner for a mutual orientation and healthy conversation to enlighten her on how she has gotten on your nerves and needed to take correction, as everyone deserves a second chance.

Then my mind was telling me to ask why it's important to set a boundary as I hummed, and he said yes, carry on. Here an unexpected smile came all over my face as I asked my friend Angelina to tell me the importance of setting boundaries.

He said that it will be important to hear this from me as I explain how vital it is once I set a boundary that helps me keep my self-respect, self-worth, mental, and emotional health in a good state.

Let me start with self-respect. What is self-respect? If I may ask you that is the question Angelina asked me.

I stammered as I tried to give a clear definition of self-respect to her, but nevertheless, I said according to my own little perspective, it can be seen as acknowledging and appreciating one's own worth, dignity, and value as a human being. It's the essence of self-respect. It entails maintaining a positive self-image, establishing boundaries, and refusing to put up with actions or circumstances that jeopardize one's morality or self-worth. Self-awareness, self-acceptance, and the capacity to assert oneself in a constructive and polite way are the cornerstones of developing self-respect. It's about treating oneself with the same respect, kindness, and compassion that one would show to others.

I must tell you that you have what it takes to make a good relationship. I keep telling people that everything is possible when you choose the right path.

Then she went further to explain these other ones to me by saying that establishing boundaries is very important when it comes to relationships. I can attest to that for maintaining your own mental and emotional well-being. When you allow people to cross your boundaries or overlook your needs, it will definitely result in feelings of frustration, leading you to ask why? This shouldn't be found in any healthy relationship, resentment, and even anger. By creating clear boundaries, you protect yourself from these negative emotions and make sure that your relationships are built on mutual respect and understanding. Finally, boundaries create a framework for healthy communication and interaction. By expressing your boundaries, you give others the chance to understand your perspective and adjust their behavior accordingly. This focuses on mutual respect and understanding within the relationship.

If you don't experience ugly situations in your relationship life, you wouldn't have a reason to ask yourself why because you have chosen a right path to building a healthy relationship.

But do you know that if for any reason you decided to share with someone your relational lifestyle and it happened that the story revolves around that you lost so much money, like thousands of dollars, which you could have used in building up and pursuing your dreams, it won't be that funny.

Since living an unexamined life and being unserious are two things that kill people's careers, the story will only leave an enduring impression of these traits.

There in the park where we sat it was as if I was lost and as well found by my friend Angelina, one more question please I asked in lonely voice how do I discover that she is a gold digger on the first date?

She nodded her head and said to me though I will say some story before I can now tell you evidences that she's a gold digger but before then hope you were the one who narrated how your friend squandered thousands of money with the friend on the first date? I said yes it was one of those things I am scared of and that was one of the reason why I throw the question because according to my friend he never knew that taking him to one of the most expensive restaurant in the city would make him to spend tones of dollar.

Consider the tale your friend shared a cautionary lesson on why letting your female friend decide the first date venue can lead to unexpected consequences. It might strain your finances or even jeopardize the friendship.

Now, let me address your question about identifying a gold digger. While there are numerous signs, a vivid example emerges from the story your friend recounted. Open your mind and eyes to grasp the essence fully I may not enumerate every characteristic, but attentive listening will unveil the telltale traits of a gold digger within the narrative I'll share.

Allow me to share a true-life story about my friend Olivia. She found joy in flaunting her material wealth, often boasting about her extravagant lifestyle and how she preferred partners who shared her love for luxury. She believed she couldn't be with a man who didn't understand the pleasures of life to the fullest. However, despite her outward show of opulence, I knew the secrets beneath her facade.

While Olivia and I lived in New York City, we weren't particularly close. She possessed all the attributes of a captivating woman, making it impossible for anyone to overlook her charm and beauty. As I observed her lavish lifestyle, I began to question our friendship. I wondered if I should follow her path, tempted by the allure of luxury living.

Upon reflection, I realized that living luxuriously isn't inherently wrong. However, true enjoyment comes from earning such a lifestyle and being able to sustain it without constant questioning or dependence on others. It's about having the means to indulge in luxury without losing sight of the effort it takes to attain and maintain such a lifestyle.

Through extensive research, I've discovered that nothing is impossible for someone who starts their day at 5:00 am and works tirelessly until dusk. By doing so, one can create any lifestyle they desire without constantly questioning why. However, pursuing a lavish lifestyle at 5:00 am without taking the necessary steps towards achieving your dreams can lead to moments of introspection and doubt by 5:00 pm. fortunately, there are strategies to achieve such a lifestyle if you have ambitious dreams and avoid distractions that could lead to regrets later.

One evening, while scrolling through my phone gallery and reminiscing about summer vacation, I stumbled upon a picture with my friend Olivia. Seeing that picture brought a smile to my face as I continued browsing through the memories. Suddenly, my phone rang, and to my surprise, it was Olivia calling. We exchanged greetings, catching up on each other's lives. Olivia mentioned she was nearby and suggested hanging out since it was the weekend. Although she didn't reveal the reason for her visit, I agreed, eager to reconnect and spend time together.

Not long ago, a doorbell rang it was my friend Olivia. I welcomed her warmly and she made herself confortable on the couch, handing her the TV remote. However, she suggested we visit a newly launched restaurant nearby. I quickly dressed and applied some body spray, which she complimented. We then hailed a taxi that dropped us off at the restaurant.

Inside, Olivia ordered a glass of red wine and began sharing her day, seeking an escape from her thoughts. She mentioned a new neighbor she had been crushing on since her breakup with Nickola. Despite her hesitation, she was drawn to him, hoping for a different outcome than her past heartbreak.

Reflecting on my own experiences, I recalled a recent encounter with the same guy. One morning, during my routine workout, I stumbled and he came to my aid, showing concern for my well-being. His kindness and charm left an impression on me, and I found myself admiring more than just his looks it was the connection and care he showed.

As he helped me home, the snowy weather adding a touch of serenity to the moment, I appreciated his genuine concern, we shared a brief conversation before he bid me farewell, leaving me with a warm memory of our interaction.

As soon as he left, my heart leaped, and I found myself wondering if I had already fallen for him. It seemed surreal, considering all I had been through with Nikola. How could those memories fade so easily, especially when the images from that time felt like they happened just yesterday? No, that couldn't be the case.

Can I continue dwelling in the past, clinging to memories that are now mere echoes of what once was? It's time to move forward, to embrace the journey of life where each encounter writes its own story, be it good or bad. What lessons will this moment with Josh bring? Will it be a tale of joy or regret?

I can't let fear hold me back. If I don't give this a chance, how will I know what lies ahead? Maybe it's time to open my heart to friendship once more after all, there's no harm in trying.

Then, on a Friday evening around 8:30 pm, the reality of my situation hit me. Tomorrow was Saturday, my usual day for exercise. Lost in thought, I received a call from Josh Gilbert, setting up a meeting at the spot where we first met. The anticipation of possibly falling in love again made my heart race. I headed to the kitchen for some sliced fruit before bed, unable to shake off the excitement.

In my dreams, love stories danced through my mind, a bittersweet fantasy. By 4:35 am, I was up, ready for my workout, changing my body spray to feel fresh. Trying to distract myself with Netflix, I couldn't focus. Thoughts of

Josh consumed me, and I dropped my phone, lost in reverie until sleep carried me away.

Awakening to the sound of missed calls from Josh at 5:56 am, panic set in. I rushed to meet him, apologizing for oversleeping. We engaged in exercise together, the morning air alive with possibilities. Josh then surprised me with a date invitation to one of the city's finest restaurants, a choice that left me both nervous and excited.

The day of our agreed-upon date arrived, and I hurried to a nearby boutique, splurging on an expensive outfit worth $15,000, a luxurious body spray for $1,000, and jewelry totaling $2,000. I was filled with excitement as I prepared for the evening.

Josh pulled up in his latest Sewell, and I eagerly awaited his call. As he arrived, he opened the car door and gestured for me to take a seat. We headed to the restaurant of my choice, where we settled into a cozy café.

Despite my nerves, I tried to charm Josh with a sweet smile and subtle gestures. However, as the conversation progressed, my true attitude and desires began to surface.

I found myself boasting about my lavish lifestyle and desires, sharing stories of luxury living and extravagant dreams like visiting Gustavia, St. Barts. Josh listened politely, but I could sense a growing unease in his demeanor.

When the waitress handed us menus, I ordered without considering the context of our first date a pricey appetizer at $75 and a lobster at $125, showcasing my expectation for extravagance without hesitation.

In my eagerness to impress Josh with my wealth and status, I painted a picture of excess and indulgence, hoping for validation through material possessions.

However, as the evening concluded and the bill was settled, I noticed a change in Josh's mood. With a polite but firm farewell, he excused himself, leaving me alone to contemplate the missed opportunity and the realization that flaunting material wealth isn't always the path to genuine connection.

Reflecting on my first date with him, I found myself asking why. Was it my extravagant lifestyle that intimidated Josh? Could this be something I could change? Was there room for improvement in my attitude?

In my pursuit of material wealth, I overlooked the significance of a genuine connection. It's the initial impression that often determines whether a bond deepens or fades into obscurity. I failed to recognize the value of being appreciated for who I am, not just for what I possess.

My friend Olivia shared a similar experience, acknowledging her past mistakes and the realization that material wealth doesn't equate to genuine happiness. She advised me to simplify things on dates, avoiding ostentatious displays that overshadow genuine connections.

As I sat alone, contemplating my choices, I questioned if my relentless pursuit of wealth had cost me true happiness. I now understand that love cannot be bought it must be earned through sincerity and humility.

I encouraged Olivia not to rush into conclusions but to understand Josh's perspective before making decisions. Not all encounters are the same, and it's important not to judge based on past experiences alone.

In conclusion, let's learn from our experiences and approach relationships with an open heart, knowing that genuine connections transcend materialistic desires.

CHAPTER ONE

THE ROLE OF ACCEPTANCE IN PERSONAL GROWTH

What can we truly accept, and when is acceptance warranted? Is it possible to accept that nobody loves us more than we love ourselves? Can concrete examples shed light on this concept?

If such facts were widely acknowledged, many individuals might find liberation from various aspects of their lives where they feel stagnant.

Consider the post-parenting phase besides our parents, who else has demonstrated profound love for us? Can we acknowledge that our spouses, partners, or significant others have also shown us such unwavering affection? How do we come to terms with the reality that no one else has loved us unconditionally?

Perhaps no one has ever fully conveyed to you the sacrifices your parents made when you were a little child. I often imagine if every trial they endured while raising you was captured in a video, you, now as an adult, would truly grasp the depth of their dedication.

From your infancy to this moment of adulthood, reflect on the unparalleled love your biological parents showered upon you. Consider the immense effort it takes for parents to nurture a child who is unaware of their own existence.

Consider asking your mother about her experiences raising you as a child. It's a poignant reminder of the bond forged in those early years.

It's unfortunate if circumstances have distanced you from your parents, be it due to divorce or death. If they have passed, may their souls rest in peace?

Do you realize the countless sacrifices your parents made before you reached adulthood? They spent sleepless nights comforting your cries, singing lullabies until you drifted into dreams.

As you grew, they stood as unwavering pillars of support, rejoicing in your every success, whether small victories like your first day of school or bigger milestones like winning a spelling bee or learning to ride a bike. Their joy for you was unceasing, always aiming to bring a smile to your face, even amidst their own struggles.

You are my sunshine, my only sunshine.

I love you to the moon and back.

You make my heart happy.

You are amazing just the way you are.

You are my greatest blessing.

You are so special to me.

I'm so proud of you.

You are the light of my life.

You are capable of achieving anything.

You are loved more than you'll ever know.

Reflecting on the words of praise like "great Mom" and "Dad" bestowed upon us in our youth, we realize the depth of sincerity in every utterance. These words stem from the depths of their hearts, minds, and spirits. While friends may speak powerful words, often they lack the profound authenticity rooted in parental love.

Consider this a true friend's expressions of love may echo the sentiments your parents once shared, especially when you were yet to grasp their full meaning. Yet, despite their efforts, these words often fall short of the depth and significance carried by a parent's words.

You mean the world to me.

I cherish every moment we spend together.

Your happiness is my priority.

I'm grateful to have you in my life.

You inspire me to be a better person.

I believe in you and your dreams.

I'll always be here for you, no matter what.

You bring so much joy and positivity into my life.

I love you more than words can express.

You're not just my friend; you're family to me.

But yet, you still see those your friends that loved you so much do this kind of things I will mention now to you.

Lying

Betrayal of Confidence

Backstabbing

Breaking Promises

Disloyalty

Manipulation

Ignoring Boundaries

Jeopardizing Safety

But it wasn't just the happy moments that defined their love. When you faced challenges and setbacks, your parents were your rock. They wiped away your tears, offered comforting words, and stood by your side through every storm. They taught you the value of strength that comes from facing adversity with love and determination.

As you grew into a young adult, you realized the depth of your parents' love. It wasn't just the hugs and kisses or the material gifts they gave you, it was the sacrifices they made, the late-night worries, and the unwavering support that spoke volumes. Their love was a constant presence in your life, shaping you into the confident and compassionate person you had become.

Years passed, and you ventured out into the world, forging your own path. Yet, no matter where life took you, the love of your parents remained a guiding light. In moments of doubt or loneliness, you would close your eyes and feel the warmth of your parents' love surrounding you, reassuring you that no matter what, you were cherished beyond measure. And in those moments, you knew with certainty that no one had ever loved you more than your biological parents, and no one ever would.

Do you realize that the primary reason for your existence today does not stem from being superior to those whose biological parents consented to their abortion while they were still developing in the womb?

It's improbable that you wouldn't exist today if your parents had not loved you. Even if they had considered aborting you, it's essential to acknowledge that your existence is a result of their decisions and circumstances.

Mind you that in life, there may be acquaintances or peers who, despite your maturity and age, might not hesitate to harm you if they had the means and opportunity. They would act decisively without hesitation.

See how important it's to follow relationships and situations with awareness and caution, recognizing that not everyone may have your best interests at heart.

This will remind you of the cherished words spoken by your friends during moments of celebration, whether it was your birthday, small achievements, or significant successes that warranted joyous recognition.

Congratulations

You mean the world to me.

I cherish every moment we spend together.

Your happiness is my priority.

I'm grateful to have you in my life.

You inspire me to be a better person.

I believe in you and your dreams.

I'll always be here for you, no matter what.

You bring so much joy and positivity into my life.

I love you more than words can express.

You're not just my friend you're family to me.

Let's take a look at the impact of words spoken by friends, considering potential scenarios that might precede their expression. However, it's important not to misconstrue their intentions. While their words may momentarily bring joy, is accepting them indicative of 75% of their affection? I have my doubts.

Refusing to accept such words is justified, as they fall short of the three-quarters love rate that parents typically share with their children.

CONGRATULATIONS

It's essential to recognize that when friends offer congratulations, there's often a good reason behind it. Anderson recently shared on his timeline that he successfully completed his university course, achieving top honors in the faculty of sciences with a CGP of 4.5. This notable achievement sparked a wave of congratulatory messages from friends and family alike, showcasing Anderson's pride in his academic success.

Anyone who comes across such a milestone, regardless of personal acquaintance, understands the immense effort and dedication required to attain such academic excellence. It's only natural, then, for individuals familiar with Anderson's journey, including former classmates and close friends, to extend their heartfelt congratulations. This collective acknowledgment of Anderson's achievement signifies the "Recognition of Achievement" phase, where awareness of his accomplishment prompts a celebration among peers.

Anderson's call for celebration invites reflection on the nature of support and acknowledgment. While many express their joy and admiration publicly, the depth of genuine support may vary. It's very important to understand that not all who extend congratulations may offer substantial assistance or ongoing support. Anderson's potential future endeavors, whether seeking financial aid or pursuing specialized projects, could reveal the true extent of support from his network.

Experiencing success and its accompanying challenges also involves understanding the nuances of relationships. Celebrating personal victories is empowering, yet remaining mindful of potential shifts in support dynamics is equally important. As Anderson experiences the ebb and flow of reactions from friends, he gains valuable directives into the complexities of human connections and the realities of navigating both success and setbacks.

Ultimately, Anderson's path serves as a reminder to cherish genuine support, remain remarkable in the face of challenges, and discern those who celebrate success authentically from those who may harbor ulterior motives. Building a network based on trust, empathy, and mutual respect ensures a robust foundation for personal and professional growth, regardless of the highs and lows encountered along the way.

To reduce the way you all ask why?

YOU MEAN THE WORLD TO ME

When it comes to relationships, familiar sentiments often surface, spoken in tender moments by our significant others Phrases like "You mean the world to me" may resonate deeply, yet the question remains, can one truly accept unconditional love? While the initial response might be affirmative, it's categorically important to tread cautiously, for such declarations can sometimes mask underlying uncertainties.

Reflecting on the complexities of romantic entanglements prompts contemplation, how does one go through the complexities of love and devotion without succumbing to doubt or confusion? It's a step by step many undertake, not without its moments of joy and bewilderment.

Consider the story of Sarah and Alex, childhood friends whose bond went beyond time and trials. Their idyllic camaraderie forged amid serene landscapes and shared dreams, was a testament to enduring friendship. One fateful day, Sarah, brimming with anticipation, presented Alex with a cherished heirloom a vintage pocket watch steeped in sentimental value.

Amid Alex's grateful astonishment, the question lingered, why this gift of profound significance? Sarah's gentle explanation unveiled layers of affection and appreciation, symbolizing their unbreakable connection and mutual admiration. The exchange encapsulated the essence of genuine companionship and heartfelt gestures, reinforcing the notion that love manifests in myriad forms.

However, as their story of love unfolds, challenges surface, testing the very foundation of their bond. Alex's introspective query is this what love looks like? Echoes the inherent complexities of relationships, where moments of doubt and introspection coexist with moments of profound connection.

In essence, the narrative of Sarah and Alex encapsulates the nuanced dynamics of love and friendship, reminding all of us that amidst life's uncertainties, genuine affection endures, offering solace and strength in moments of vulnerability.

Alex believed Sarah was the one he would spend his life with, and Sarah cherished their bond as well. However, one fateful day, everything changed.

Sarah began spending more time away from Alex, often citing work or other commitments. Alex noticed the growing distance but dismissed it, trusting Sarah completely. Unbeknownst to him, Sarah had started seeing another man behind his back.

Initially oblivious, Alex was blinded by love and missed the signs. Over time, the truth unraveled. He discovered Sarah's lies about her where about, he came across messages hinting at an affair on her phone, and heard rumors from mutual friends.

Confronting Sarah about his suspicions shattered Alex's world. Sarah initially denied but later confessed to cheating on him. The betrayal cut deep, leaving Alex devastated and questioning their entire relationship.

Days filled with tears, arguments, and emotional turmoil followed. Alex struggled to accept that someone he trusted had betrayed him at all cost. Despite the pain, he chose to let go, recognizing the toxicity of a relationship built on lies.

Walking away, Alex carried lessons of trust, betrayal, and self-love, vowing to protect himself from such hurt in the future. Stories like his are sadly common, highlighting the challenges of love and trust in relationships and marriages.

But how do we avoid such heartbreak? Does it mean avoiding relationships altogether? It's essential not to overlook red flags or compromise on self-respect for the sake of a relationship. Life's stages often teach us invaluable lessons, telling us to view each phase with wisdom and self-preservation, rather than dwelling on unanswered 'why' questions.

EMBRACE CHANGE IN EVERY PHASE OF LIFE

Cultivate a Growth Mindset looking at challenges as opportunities for growth and learning is very important. It's about seeing setbacks as temporary hurdles and extracting valuable lessons from them.

Consider this, When faced with adversity, questioning why certain friends might revel in your misfortune can be a stumbling block. It can divert your attention from the valuable lessons that both success and failure phases offer.

Every phase of life presents its unique opportunities. Dwelling too much on the negative aspects of past experiences often leads to one question: Why? However, dwelling on 'why' tends to tether you to the past without offering substantial insights for moving forward.

In such moments, there might be no one to stand by you and explain why certain friends celebrated your downfall. Perhaps their celebration stemmed from a lack of genuine care or their own unresolved issues.

Instead of dwelling on their motives, consider this, what can you learn from this situation to create, focus on personal growth and avoid similar pitfalls in the future? By shifting your focus to constructive actions and self-improvement, you redirect your energy towards positive outcomes.

This shift not only alleviates regrets but also create a way for future successes that will be celebrated on a global scale.

If you don't realize that nothing lasts forever and that adaptation is important, how do you believe life itself will be flexible? Be flexible and receptive to new things. Realize that life is dynamic and that being adaptable lets you deal with unforeseen circumstances. If your parents, who were your pillar of support, have already passed away, may they rest in peace and know that you have no one to turn to in a moment like this. Why is it even necessary for you to keep in mind that some people are late and that you cannot make it without them?

It's clear that you've adjusted to the fact that you must pursue your goals on your own without assistance and that you're receptive to new experiences that are right in front of you but that you are unable to change right now. But keep in mind that every circumstance life throws at you presents you fresh opportunities and challenges, so you still have the option to make a change and, if you can, take a vacation. You will gain new experience and pick up where you left off by doing this.

Not how far you've come, but the modest steps toward success you take every day of your life are what matter most.

Nobody is going to monitor your development, so accept that you are not making as much progress as you could be in your current circumstances, even though you are still doing your hardest.

Nobody will doubt your current state of advancement if you spend about three hours a day improving yourself, reading a ton of books, and gaining knowledge that will help you realize your dreams. I can speak to that because I am a living example of it.

I'm hoping that after reading this book, you will get me a gift because I've learned valuable lessons from life that you and other people like I myself can use to writing. Which sports are you truly skilled at? Do you love football? I assume you've heard of Lionel Messi and Cristiano Ronaldo by now, or do you like swimming?

Many persons who have broken records and are capable of more currently include Michael Phelps and Katie Ledecky, who are well-known for their wrestling careers. I'll tell you, you can look up their records and history, which most of them have retained. You'll all know by then that the majority of those individuals never maintained such records overnight.

The length of time or hours needed to become a professional in any field can vary greatly depending on a number of factors, including the field's complexity, each learner's unique learning style, level of dedication, and opportunities for hands-on experience. A professional in a field usually needs to study, practice, and apply their talents in the actual world for several years.

For instance, to be recognized as a professional, one must typically complete several years of formal education, practical training, internships, and professional exams in professions including academics, engineering, medicine, law, and engineering. This can sometimes last up to ten years or longer.

The time required to become a professional can be shortened in some industries, such as software development, graphic design, or digital marketing. These fields often require a few years of education or independent study mixed with real-world experience gained through internships, projects, and ongoing learning.

In the end, developing one's skills, gaining real-world experience, and remaining current with industry advancements are all necessary on the path to becoming a professional in any sector.

Then keep in mind that everyone has an area in which their interests are primarily concentrated. If this is the case, you already know where your thoughts are going, so you don't need confirmation from others that your goals are attainable. In light of this, you will take the following actions to succeed in the field on which you are basing your dreams.

However, if your dream is to work as a software engineer, it's possible that you've heard of people who have achieved incredible success in that industry, that you've kept a close eye on yourself, and that you've trusted in yourself enough to not just tell yourself lies. Grinning, do you think that sounds absurd? It does occur. People have the ability to deceive themselves since there exist individuals in various academic fields, although most of them are well aware that they don't fit, are there nonetheless because they fell in love with those who are amazing at what they do. They may have looked within and discovered they are not very excellent in that area, but since they have known people who have excelled in that area. That is not how things ought to be. In order to begin the process of telling yourself the truth about your entire life, you must first acknowledge who you are. To do this, thoroughly search your thoughts to identify the areas in which you excel.

You know full well that you are performing well in the game of soccer you cannot be playing like Lionel Messi and yearn to become a medical doctor.

Did I convey myself clearly? A life without reflection is not worth living. It is entirely true, even though Socrates said it first and I never did. Establishing objectives for every stage of your life is strength of acceptance that everyone ought to know. What does that mean? It basically means that if you get up every day without having made any goals, you are putting your life in jeopardy and living contrary to Socrates's dictum on humility.

A person must establish and specify specific objectives for every stage of his life. Unless he lacks the determination to lead a virtuous life, which will serve as inspiration and guidance when someone talks about motivations and directions, what specifically comes to mind? For example, suppose you are among fifty students in your class and you are declared the top graduating student. How will you feel? That's an example, but in reality, you'll feel good about yourself and inspired to work more in your studies in order to achieve greater academic success.

Now explain to me how a student can be the best graduating student without having a schedule that tells him when to study a certain subject, when to relax, when to get some sleep, when to get some exercise, and when to hang out with friends. After all, work without play truly makes a person dull.

Don't make it appear as though I'm telling a parable. You deserve to be better and make better use of your time by realizing how important it is to set goals when working on a project. Let's take the following example, you are a software developer working on a major project and you have realized that you have a daily schedule, perhaps for a friend's visit, and that after that time you might not be able to complete a goal you have set for the day. It's possible that by that point you haven't fully realized the consequences of falling short of your daily goals.

Say "know and strategize," instead. Perhaps you were meant to complete the software within the allotted six months, but before you know it, your everyday obligations prevent you from following your objective as it was outlined. In this case, you may begin to blame yourself and ask why you are not doing the tasks that are expected   of   you. What's the issue? There will be questions, but I'll tell you right now that you are the source of your own issues. Why don't you accept that goal-setting and sticking to it are two of acceptance's strengths by removing any other obstacles that stand in the way of accomplishing each daily objective that you have set for yourself? If your schedules are the primary cause of your inability to meet as planned, you must realize that if you truly mean and believe the project is an integral element of your ambition and profession, you can attend to those Schedules some other time.

Days when you don't accomplish your stated goals for the day are already working against your dream and career, just like every other thing you do. Time is money, as they say, and money is time, so you have to be careful with when you let money in and out so that it can continue to work for you even while you're asleep.

Then, how do you make a goal and stick with it? These are the steps you need to take to accomplish each daily objective.

REFLECT ON VALUES

Choose your core principles first. These are the principles and ideals that guide your decisions and actions. Knowing what matters most to you will make it simpler to set meaningful goals that align with your beliefs.

As a software engineer, discovering your core values means thinking about the principles, goals, and values that guide your decisions and actions, but before you can do that, there are a few important things you need to do.

Make a list of the things that are most important to you and consider the situations, ideas, or past experiences that have had a significant influence on you.

It's also important to set priorities for your job, relationships, personal growth, and community service. In this sense, you will determine when to reach your life's objectives in order to avoid interfering with other aspects of your life. You should all applaud yourselves for taking this action, in my opinion, as the results will be outstanding.

There is also the method of defining principles. Clarify the values that you hold dear and wish to follow in both your personal and professional life after you have defined the principle. Integrity, honesty, creativity, teamwork, and social responsibility are a few of them.

Remember that you are the only one who can arrange your life the way you see fit there must be a purpose behind your decision to do so. You have every right to do so. It doesn't matter what other people say about how you chose to define those values, what matters is how well they align with your own standard of living. After all, what other people believe isn't usually better for you in any area of your life, be it relationships, education, mental health, or even finances.

Have I already told you that nobody really gives a damn about how well you live your life? Hear it now, and get ready for it. Nobody gives a damn because, if I'm not mistaken, if you believe that even your closest buddy can be of assistance to you, things might not work out well in the end since you might experience disappointment.

Evaluate acts: Determine whether the choices and acts you've made in the past are consistent with your ideals. Describe times when you felt happy or satisfied with yourself because what you did was in keeping with your basic   beliefs. In actuality, it is inappropriate to pursue any endeavor in life without first determining one's basic principles. Priorities should direct one's actions and decision-making in any endeavor. Regardless of your occupation medical professional, cab driver, affiliate marketer, gynecologist, etc. Can we now take the time to investigate the facts that must be taken into account while assessing actions? It's important as well to assess an action's effects on both oneself and other people. Every action has an impact on relationships and results they can be as simple as gestures or as complex as decisions. Here are some important factors to take into account while assessing acts.

Intent Understand the intention behind the action you have made. Was it done with good intentions, or was there a hidden agenda? Intent often plays a significant role in how actions are perceived and received by others.

Consequences Assess the potential consequences of your action. Will it lead to positive outcomes or cause harm? It's important to consider the short-term and long-term effects as that can help in making informed evaluations.

Alignment with Values Reflect on whether the action aligns with your personal values and principles. Acting in accordance with your values focuses on integrity and authenticity in relationships and decision-making.

Empathy Put yourself in the shoes of those affected by the action you take. How would they perceive it? Practicing empathy enhances understanding and promotes better communication and conflict resolution. Especially when you are into business that requires you communicate with lots of people to generate income. You have to try your possible best to see that you accommodate every single attitude you come across while having a conversation with people, as every one may not display the same pattern of attitude and that's when tolerance is needed to keep the conversation in good and healthy condition.

But you must say know when it's needed to avoid making a costly mistake that may lead to setback in any of your life phase as that is the major point we are looking into.

Feedback Seek feedback from trusted sources to gain different perspectives on the action. Because you making a decision at a time, you may not understand every aspect that the decision will not favor it When you get a feedback that will stand a chance to know if the good aspect of that decision made by you is greater than the side effect of it. Constructive feedback can provide valuable insights and guide future actions. Then definitely you will surely make another decision from the feedback you are getting from the audience.

Learn and Adapt Learn from past actions and experiences. Use feedback and reflections to adapt and improve decision-making processes over time.

Adaptation is very important but before then you still have to understand that is not what could be done overnight to adapt is a gradual process which will take a series of process to achieve. Never worry as you are not alone on that process because there are many ways through which you can follow to adapt to any situation you find yourself regardless of the field you need the adaption then we move on and I guess that we are going to talk more on that on next chapter of this book.

All this are aspect that is needed to be considering, before one can effectively evaluate actions and their implications on personal growth, relationships, and overall well-being.

Break Goals into Actionable Steps: Break down each goal into smaller, actionable steps. This makes them less daunting and helps you stay focused and motivated as you progress towards achieving them.

There's how you are meant to place your goals before they can be achievable. By making them look simple and as well breaking them into small, small parts, unless it's in such a way that you cannot break them up by yourself, it implies that you have to consult someone who has already worked on such a project or a project that's similar to the one you are about to work on. By then, you will give a listening ear to the person to get the most important thing that he has to tell you about breaking your goals in that project. Maybe it's the right time to seek mentorship and devote your time to learning and growing better in your field.

Regularly Review and Adjust: Periodically review your goals to assess your progress and make any necessary adjustments. Life is dynamic, and circumstances may change, so it's important to adapt your goals accordingly.

Certainly you are not alone always remember that reviewing your goals, will automatically draw a road map to most the things you got correct and motivate you to keep to those ones and try so much to eradicate anyone that granted you nothing but a setback.

Anyways you can as well share the review with people because if it's the one that requires that you will get a feedback from them it's important you get a review from them, let's take for instance that you making a software that is to deliver to people how to lose weight without hitting a gym house, then it's very important you share with them because if you have practiced what the software delivered and it gave you a good impression , you still need to share the software to them and give them some time to go through the software and give you some review and beware that both negative and positive review must be welcomed by you, so that you will know the specific area to adjust before the final lunch of the software. That is what regular review can do to anyone in any field you are into, regular review is very important.

Celebrate Milestones Celebrate your achievements along the way, no matter how small. This helps boost your confidence and motivation to continue pursuing your goals.

I myself celebrate every single success I make, regardless of how little it could be. I could see how crazy I could be at time I still celebrate my failure but not in a big way, because after the failure, I will always try as much as I can to sort out what led to the failure and as well try to fix it. And keep it on my record book, Do you know why it's important to also acknowledge the failure? That's because failure tells you that you are working on something and that if you don't give up, on a certain day you will get it correct and celebrate the success in a bigger way.

Then remember that you can't fail when you are not doing anything; that's one of the most important things you have to tell yourself.

Practice Self-Compassion: Be kind to yourself throughout this process. It's natural to face challenges and setbacks, but instead of dwelling on regrets or asking "why," focus on learning from experiences and using them to grow and improve.

Being kind to yourself is something that you must do to keep moving without so much regret and part of it is to always bring out to have enough rest. Make yourself happy, chill out with some friends, and don't forget to always go on vacation.

But let all those things be done in accordance with your schedules in such a way that they won't bring setbacks to you while working on a project or trying to achieve certain goals.

Life is fraught with unpredictability and concerns about what lies ahead. In a world filled with uncertainties, such as the ongoing economic fluctuations and personal challenges related to health, finances, and relationships, it's natural to yearn for stability and a sense of control. However, the reality is that much of life's journey remains shrouded in ambiguity.

The way we perceive and approach uncertainty plays a important role in how we navigate difficult circumstances and confront the unknown with confidence. Fear and uncertainty can trigger feelings of stress, anxiety, and a loss of control over our lives. This emotional burden can lead to a continuous cycle of worrying about potential outcomes and dwelling on worst-case scenarios.

Nevertheless, adopting a resilient mindset is essential for managing uncertainty effectively. Instead of succumbing to fear and worry, focus on building inner strength and adaptability. Embrace the idea that change is a constant in life and that challenges can present opportunities for growth and learning. By cultivating a positive outlook and developing coping strategies, you can empower yourself to face uncertainties with courage and resilience.

Remember, while you may not always have control over external circumstances, you have the power to shape your mindset and response to uncertainty. By cultivating a sense of inner calm and embracing the ebb and flow of life, you can navigate uncertainties with grace and confidence.

PRACTICE SELF-REFLECTION

You can't embrace the power of acceptance without considering practicing of self-reflection

At its heart, self-reflection is setting aside time to think deeply and evaluate your thoughts, attitudes, motivations, and desires. It's examining your emotions and behaviors and then asking yourself, why you feel and act this way.

You get to spend more time with yourself more than anyone else.

But this is a question that no one can ever imagine asking you, how well do you know yourself?

Being confronted with who you are is often uncomfortable. It means holding yourselves accountable, admitting your weaknesses, and trying to further your personal development. Sometimes, it seems easier to ignore anything potentially negative about yourself.

But then, you're actually less self-aware than you think. Many people believe they're self-aware, but only 10-15% of people around the globe can attest to it.

When you understand your influences, drives, and impulses, you'll have an easier time living a happy, fulfilling life. And the key to understanding yourself is self-reflection, the process of looking inward and examining your emotional responses and behaviors.

Taking the time to reflect on life might sound like a little bit of an overwhelming task to you, but I tell you, it really worth it. You might think have this act of introspection as something that naturally occurs as you grow older, but the truth be told, self-reflection can and should be practiced at any age. And it can be as simple as looking back at your behavior in any scenario to ask yourself why you behaved the way you did.

Self-reflection builds self-awareness. Did you get what I mean? But that can be achieved through intention and dedication. That is to let you know in a situation you expected to press "pause" on your busy life to create time and space to sit peacefully to sift through your thoughts and interactions to scrutinize them without judgment or condemnation.

Then, in these processes, what I do recommend for you is river banks where there are lots of trees and less noise. At least you will have all the time to yourself, and by then you will find the great teacher you could be to yourself.

Because you will surely ask yourself lots of questions after reflecting on how your life is going, no one will be with you all your life to remind you of the day you were supposed to be having a rest but omitted due to other schedules that are best known to you and you alone. But when you settle down and take out your time, you will realize all by yourself and possibly make a positive change, and by then, positive results will keep reflecting in your life over time.

It's not by mistake that I must specify to you that the value of self-reflection lies in its power to help identify what's working well in your life and develop insight into what isn't and why.

Without going into introspection, you risk remaining trapped in a monotonous routine devoid of productivity or inspiration. Understanding the root of your dissatisfaction and identifying ways to enhance your circumstances becomes challenging when you lack clarity about your true desires.

When embarking on a journey of self-discovery, take it slow. Growth necessitates confronting both the positive and negative aspects of your character, yet self-examination should not lead to feelings of anxiety, stress, or depression.

If you catch yourself overanalyzing and self-criticizing excessively for past mistakes, take a step back and refocus. Introspection should foster understanding and a deeper connection with your identity, not serve as a platform for self-condemnation.

Integrate self-discovery into your daily, weekly, and monthly routines using straightforward strategies. Choose a quiet and relaxed time of day, whether it's upon waking up or before bedtime. Consistency is key stick to your chosen routine to yield meaningful results from your self-reflection practice.

Think about this few questions on your daily self-reflection questions

What can you do to take better care of yourself mentally?

What can you do to create a positive outlook on life?

What areas of your life do you feel satisfied with? Which ones need attention?

Are you taking anything in your life for granted?

What fears or worries keep you up at night?

HERE ARE SOME REPHRASED QUESTIONS TO JUMPSTART SELF-REFLECTION

What are the key values that guide your decisions and actions?

How do you handle challenges and setbacks, and what can you learn from these experiences?

In what areas of your life do you feel fulfilled, and what can you do to enhance this feeling?

What are your long-term goals, and what steps can you take today to work towards achieving them?

How do you manage stress and maintain a healthy work-life balance?

All these are valuable questions we ought to be asking ourselves on a regular basis. Maybe you should get a pen and paper to sort out possible answers to those questions according to your own point of view.

I have done mine because I place the questions on my table every morning and consider looking into them one after the other before embarking on my daily routine.

Make you continue looking into the question until you have them all off hand. That will assist you in meditating on the answer you have crafted for yourself every day and trying to make good use of those answers.

SELF-REFLECTION JOURNALING EXERCISES

List 5 things that make you smile and identify the reason behind them.

What are three things you are grateful for today, and why?

What emotions did you experience today, and how did they affect your thoughts and actions?

What are your top priorities for the upcoming week, and how can you stay focused on them?

In what ways did you show kindness or support to others today, and how did it make you feel?

Maybe it's the right time to pick a pen and paper, as it will really sound ok if you can put most of those answers in your book and keep looking at them over time. If there are some areas where you are not getting it right by memorizing it, you will all have to make an effort and keep moving forward.

CHAPTER 2

CULTIVATING RESILIENCE THROUGH ACCEPTANCE OF LIFE'S CHALLENGES

Life is a journey, an unexpected one full of ups and downs. Who on earth can honestly claim never to have encountered obstacles in life in a variety of forms? I personally am afraid to even state such a thing, as I think life is full of ups and downs. But since our goal should be to remain focused on chasing our objectives in many areas of life, how can we endure those ups and downs without questioning why?

Perhaps I should reiterate this, although obstacles are an unavoidable aspect of life, they should serve as a reminder that how you handle them and how you choose to react to them ultimately determines who you are as a person and how your future turns out. Then come the necessary ingredients for conquering obstacles in life perseverance, resilience, and an optimistic outlook.

I promise you that no matter what kind of difficulty life throws at you, if you embrace resilience and have an optimistic outlook, you will overcome it. If it's alright with you, let's take each of those stages in turn, since they will help us overcome any obstacles life may present.

Accepting that difficulties are an inherent part of the human experience should be your first priority. You should take those challenges as they are and try not to worry too much about them. Remember that you cannot solve every problem in life on your own. Perhaps if you come into such a situation, remember that you are not alone and try not to panic. To obtain all the information needed to take on the challenge, all you have to do is relax, give it some time, and ask a few questions.

By acknowledging and accepting this truth, you can establish a growth-oriented mindset in which you view challenges as chances to learn new things and further your own development. Recognize that you possess the strength and ability to persevere through challenging circumstances and emerge from them stronger.

Breaking problems down into smaller, more achievable steps is important to preventing emotions of helplessness and inaction. You can approach the task more easily and build momentum by remembering to take things one step at a time and appreciating every little accomplishment along the way. You cannot ignore the need of breaking down obstacles into doable steps if you want to develop resilience and a positive outlook on life.

From your own perspective, how do you view resilience? Perhaps I should repeat what I said to you all. You should realize that no man is an island, that no one is an expert, and that we are all constantly learning. For this reason, you must pay attention to what I think is crucial information regarding resilience, and you should also accept it. Since it's among the most effective strategies for overcoming obstacles in life

It is not their fault that some people do not have the time to explore useful words from a dictionary, many people are too busy with their daily activities to have much time to go through their dictionary.

I don't think it's necessary to use a lot of words to explain resilience clearly, so I'll just put it down as briefly as possible. Hopefully you can understand what I'm saying.

Resilience is the ability to withstand adversity and setbacks.

Instead, focus on creating coping mechanisms and techniques for reducing stress in order to promote resilience. Engage in activities that support your mental and emotional well-being, such as writing, exercise, and mindfulness. By strengthening your resilience, you'll be able to handle stress better and bounce back from setbacks faster.

Can you seriously consider the idea of building resilience through accepting life as it is and adopting a growth mindset? Not every challenge you face will make you feel frustrated in fact, some may even test your mettle and pave the way for your greater success. So why are you afraid of challenges rather than building resilience?

It is important that I bring you back to things that I have already mentioned since they are once again necessary. Recognize that failure is not a reflection of your worth, but rather an opportunity for learning.

When you face challenges in life, think about the lessons you can take away from them and how you can use those lessons to go forward in your life.

It will look so boring if we don't look into steps on how to build resilience while working on a project.

A project cannot be developed without a clear understanding of its goal. That seems fantastic since it could encourage feelings of commitment, zeal, and excitement for your work. Additionally, by aligning your personal and professional goals, it might make you feel more content.

Perhaps you ought to, now is the perfect moment to take

advantage of your alone time, unwind, and list all the reasons why that project ought to succeed.

What precisely is the project offering to people, or are you attempting to start a business? Don't you think that the first question that should cross your mind is where is this project taking me, and will it be beneficial to you if I succeed in realizing my dreams? Perhaps it would be best for you to remain composed, figure things out on your own, and trust your intuition before asking others who have gone before you for guidance.

However, did you realize that finding a mentor ideally, someone who is familiar with the nature of your ideal project is important? If you had truly discovered your mission by then, I believe that you may have thought of a question of this kind.

Perhaps I should instill in you the idea that you should think carefully about the amount of danger you are willing to accept in order to realize your ambition.

If the risk is worth taking

Manage your emotions

Embrace change and uncertainty

Practice self-care and gratitude

Learn from your experience

The ability to embrace and acknowledge reality without resistance or judgment is mostly what we overlook, but basically it involves accepting oneself, others, and situations as they appear without making any changes or wishing to have total control over them.

Then you may wonder, how do you tackle this challenge? Yes, "it's normal to just do it.

But when you allow it to take total control over your mind and some other thing that doesn't have anything to do with it, it will harm your emotions, dreams, and physical health and probably destroy the way you relate to people.

If you discover early that getting worried about situations you can't change immediately by yourself won't be of good help to you, then you will realize how far you may have gone after the challenge has been resolved.

You have to accept things the way they appear, not because you don't deserve better, but because when you accept, you will feel much better, such that stress will be reduced, your mental well-being will improve, you will have better relationships, and you will have increased resilience.

Watch yourself, and maybe you should tell yourself that whenever you are stressed, you are always better. Maybe that is a lie that you keep telling yourself, and I have never heard anyone say that you keep enjoying stress, and stress does contribute awesomely well to his personal life growth.

If you feel bad whenever you get stressed out, then know that it's not good for your growth from any perspective of your life. One can get stressed out after a trip for vacation and also for engaging in his usual daily schedules that's normal. But how well does your life matter to you, especially when it comes to physical health?

Reflect on this one's again and whisper to yourself what you feel like after reflecting on it.

Mental health encompasses a state of well-being that empowers individuals to cope with life's challenges, discover their capabilities, excel in learning and work, and contribute positively to their communities. It is a fundamental aspect of overall health and wellness, supporting your capacity to make decisions, foster relationships, and shape your environment. Mental health represents a fundamental human entitlement and plays a vital role in personal growth, community cohesion, and socio-economic progress.

Beyond merely the absence of mental disorders, mental health manifests along a multifaceted spectrum, varying in intensity and impact from person to person. This spectrum entails diverse experiences, ranging from manageable difficulties to significant distress, with potential differences in social and clinical consequences.

Mental health conditions encompass a range of states, including mental disorders, psychosocial disabilities, and other mental states marked by substantial distress, impaired functioning, or a risk of self-harm. It should be made known to you that individuals with mental health conditions may often face challenges in maintaining optimal mental well-being, this is not universally or inevitably the case.

How often do you visit the hospital and have you for one day think and as well ask why thousands of people keep being admitted into the psychiatric department? Have you ever visited psychiatrists for concealment? I guess by now you should have known that mental health is very, very important. People with mental issues often don't function effectively until they receive medications and probably take a gradual process that is required to finally recover well from it.

Then why don't you take full precaution now that you are aware that stress is one of those things that cause mental health issues and that it can also limit you from so many things, such as your state of happiness?

Although things may happen to you, if you do not know that accepting them the way they appear immediately is the very first step to take, you will hurt yourself.

Meanwhile, I don't know whether you have ever felt this way that I felt when I lost my lovely pet, a Rottweiler dog by the name Jimmy. I felt totally bad, everything was upside down to me that day, and I was beginning to ask myself why Jimmy.

Not quite long ago, I discovered that the only thing that can help me is to totally accept that my lovely pet is gone and move on.

My own experience of what got me both physically and emotionally down was the death of my lovely dog Jimmy, while yours may be a different thing all together.

Then tell me if it happened that your company was raised down by a fire incident, what exactly would be your reaction within a month after the incident, or that you lost your loved one, maybe your lovely mom, your one and only child, or how about you seeing your most favorable artist die in the code hand of death? So many things could happen to anyone at different moments, but the question is, how do you accept whatever comes your way without being hurt both mentally, emotionally, and most importantly physically?

Meanwhile, you and I understand that it's not that easy to accept, but remember that nothing will happen on earth and it will be tagged as new.

The only thing is that it may occur in different dimensions.

While accepting misfortune might be difficult, it's a necessary step in developing resilience and making constructive progress.

Where the acceptance should start?

Such is the quest that you ought to ask yourself as it a gradual process that needs proper attention to handle.

But can you now take time to know the actual step to follow while you accept anything that may befall you in life. Be it that you are sick or that you are been diagnosed of deadly disease your doctor on his own has tried giving you a precaution measure to take and you still have a little doubt in your mind, this exactly what you should do basically many has been saved from getting hurt over years for taking this steps. This is to let you know that you are not always alone in the journey of life if only you can take it easy on yourself.

Then, let's take a look at those steps one after the other.

First things first, you should have it in your mind that you are having unusual feelings in you, though it's normal to feel that way, but maybe by accepting your emotions about the misfortune. Allow you to feel sad, angry, or disappointed without judgment.

But you may not know when and at what time you have accepted it. Who is to tell you that you have already accepted it? You, yourself, are the best person to tell yourself that, if you accept the misfortune, even when you remember that something happened, you won't feel bad by being angry or disappointed without judgment.

I told you that it's a gradual process, and you have to start by acknowledging your feelings. You may not even be able to describe how you feel, but the truth is that with time, everything will fall back and you will begin to feel better and ok.

Like I said earlier, nothing will happen now. Here it is the first time of it happening, so why are you feeling so bad and getting depressed? Maybe you are addicted to drugs and you have been fighting it all alone. I have to let you know that you can't even remember how it all started or how you got into it, but you can do it by getting to know that it's hurting your life and at the same time understand that you can quite it someday as people have already been audited and someday they testified.

You too can testify if only you can accept it the way it appears in your life right now and believe that it will come to an end.

Maybe I should tell you that nothing lasts forever, maybe it's time you consider most of the things that you do, and lots of joy follows in you while you do them. More especially, things that entertain you whenever you are less busy. At first, remember that there's a reason why you need to be happy at that particular moment, which should be based on the misfortune that befalls you. If you practice the art of being happy at all times, it will automatically become part of you. That will help you so much. Know that it must not necessarily mean that you will practice that whenever you encounter a challenge in life, it's just a process that you need to take in order to accept any kind of predicament.

As soon as the sun sets, there must be a story to tell. If you don't have a story to tell today, it definitely won't escape to be told tomorrow. The story may be the one that can gladden your heart, or it could be the one that makes you frighten your face. Who told you that you wouldn't learn from any of those stories?

Maybe you didn't capture the story well, and that's why you were unable to learn from it, or maybe it was never an interesting one, but that shouldn't be a good reason why you didn't learn from it.

Life is a story on its own. When you doubt that life is not a story on its own, I may not say that you are lying, but it's a big fact. If you must know about people, then it's either you read through their memo and that will review to you most of the things that they have been through in their life.

Be it that the person is alive or late, there must be an area where they will tell a true life story of the person you are reading through his memo, which may somehow sound bitter, but if it's someone like Prince Harry, you will still come to a place where he encountered challenges in his life yet he conquered them. So, what am I saying? There are prominent people, and if they share their life story today, you will come to realize that no one is bigger than others when it comes to facing a life challenge.

But what matters is how they were able to handle the so-called life problems. When they occur, you are not different from them; the only thing is that you aren't practicing self-compassion.

Maybe at this point in time, you are ready to practice self-compassion to make a different change in your entire life. Be kind and understanding towards yourself during difficult times. Practice self-compassion by treating yourself with the same care and empathy you would offer to a friend facing a similar situation. By doing so, time will have an effect on your life?

Here, you're down one moment and up the next. It's akin to ascending a mountain without a map. It requires perseverance, fortitude, and support from those around you. You'll probably run against obstacles along the path. But ultimately, you go to the summit and realize how far you've come.

Try to shift your perspective on the misfortune by looking for potential silver linings or lessons to be learned. While it may not diminish the impact of the misfortune, reframing it in a positive light can help you accept it more effectively.

In a healthy relationship, one partner may exhibit animalistic behavior, thereby making the other feel bad, and it can even weigh one down. But then, how do you handle issues like that or close-related ones?

In a moment that you feel bad, the power to conquer is in your hands, but that will not just happen if you don't follow the normal process, which is shifting your perspectives from that which got you upset.

Maybe it's time to hang out with a friend and have some good time, take some relief, and think about how to be a better version of yourself, No one knows your story more than you yourself, and that is one of the major reasons why you should absolutely live, not give an atom of fuck.

Learn that the only thing that's constant in life is change, and if the need arises that you should make a change, never delay, for such is normal. And that is the essence of shifting your perspective whenever you feel so depressed over a particular issue that tends to deprive you of joy, happiness, good health, and all that does not contribute to the positive growth of your lifestyle.

Focus on What You Can Control

The worst thing that can happen to a man is wasting time trying to control things that are not within his reach at a particular point in time. It may be that you have not noticed when you wasted some of your precious time doing such a thing, but never mind, even though it's a tiny habit that you are struggling with already and you are not aware of it, for sure it won't last forever provided that you are making a move to get rid of it.

Maybe you have figured out that there was a time you tried so hard to manage your anger without taking proper steps towards that, or maybe you have discovered how much you have gained weight. People who suddenly get obsessed do think that it's their entire fault, and they are always looking for a way to improve their fitness. At times, they keep thinking about how to go about it over time. By asking lots of questions, not minding that thinking about their situation can only call for emotional unrest.

At that moment, you were thinking about your body's unusual shape, and it's getting you down emotionally and, as well, making you feel depressed. Permit me to let you understand that you are already in the state of focusing on what you can't control at that moment.

What exactly would be the side effect of that on you? Maybe you will experience mental, emotional, and physical challenges as well.

But it's a simple fact that you can fix and as well learn from, You may quickly ask yourself how and I must tell you that the reason you asked yourself why is because you never cleared the doubt in you.

Understand that accepting is to believe. Maybe you never took a bold step in your life before. Accept the fact that there are issues that are 100% not within your control but it doesn't mean there are issues you can't fix. Maybe it's time you understand that every problem has a suitable step to take and once a required step is taken, a solution will come. It may not come overnight but with time, understand it this way and have peace of mind.

Focus on things you can control nobody stands a better chance to tell you that you should have total control over your dream but in the process of pursuing your dream, a challenge that is not within your control befalls you, You shouldn't think otherwise, rather see it as the right time to re-direct your focus and think of getting the issue fixed before you continue.

Let's take a good look at this simple fact, you came back from work only to find out that your kitchen sink is seriously having a lick and maybe that you don't know the steps to take to get it fixed by yourself. Now what should first come to your mind is that I have tried fixing it by myself, but it wasn't going well. What next should you do in order to get it fixed? Maybe you should try getting in touch with a plumber whose major work is dealing with all kinds of plumbing issue. By then, I should tell you that you have taken the very bold step of getting the sink fixed to avoid the lick age, as that can disrupt your cooking.

Likewise to other problems in life, the only thing you should do is figure out the best steps to follow and tackle the issue. Once you discover the right step to follow, every other thing will become a story of another day, so you need not worry about allotting time to any problem, especially once you know quite clearly that it is not within your control.

Life can't go on without a challenge it's either a lesser challenge or a bigger one, what really matters is how you tackle any kind of challenge without giving it a chance to harm any aspect of your life.

Direct your energy towards aspects of the situation that you can control or influence. This may involve taking practical steps to address the consequences of the misfortune or making decisions that empower you to move forward.

Your life is your right, but what it takes to have a total control over it does not lie only in your hands.

You cannot be a banker and still make it a professional tailor, so where do you stand it's a question then if you are a banker whenever the need arise that you need a new dress it's either that you search for a professional that knows how to sow cloth or you look for a well-known boutique to get any kind of design that you wish.

Life won't sound fun to you if you try to take control over natural phenomenon called problems.

Life is filled with challenges waiting to be solved. Whether it's earning a living or going through personal struggles, every day presents an opportunity to overcome obstacles and make life easier. Only the lifeless escape these trials, perhaps in realms beyond our experience. So, when faced with health, physical, or emotional challenges, remember that it's part of being alive. Trust the process, believe in the process, and know that every problem has its time for resolution."

Mindfulness in place

Engaging in mindfulness practices such as meditation, deep breathing can be incredibly beneficial for staying present and grounded, especially when facing misfortune. These practices allow you to cultivate a sense of awareness and acceptance of the present moment, helping you avoid getting lost in negative thoughts or ruminations about what could have been.

Meditation, for instance, encourages focusing on the breath and observing thoughts without judgment. This can create a space between you and your emotions, allowing for a more balanced perspective on the situation. Deep breathing exercises can help calm the mind and body, reducing the stress and anxiety that often accompany challenging times.

Journaling provides a structured way to express your thoughts and feelings, allowing you to process emotions and gain clarity on your experiences. Writing down your thoughts can also help you identify patterns of thinking that may be contributing to your distress, enabling you to challenge and reframe them more effectively.

These is basically how to practice mindfulness but on your own you can take time to know if your daily schedule probably do give you up to an hour time meditation, if so what and what do you meditate on is it only when you encounter problem that you remember to meditate?

Even when you are into a business maybe the business is flourishing and you are happy with the way it's going it's nice that you have such experience but I must tell you that much meditations is also required to keep that business moving.

How do you meditate?

When are you supposed to meditate?

You meditate based on the field you are operating in, you can't be a farmer and be meditating on how to treat a psychiatric patient, if you are a farmer you meditate on how to grow your farm better and set the farm to the standard of your test and also to meet up to the satisfaction of your customer .

People who patronize you in any field you are in there satisfaction should be considered as your number one priority.

Maybe there are things that are not in order as expected by your customer and you are thinking on how to get it fixed, if you don't have a leisure time to meditate, you may probably get the step to fix it wrong.

And that is how it should be applied in all other areas of your life. In your relational life, spiritual life, and marital life, in fact, you have to sit down and look at other areas of your life that I didn't mention. Remember that where a problem may appear in your own area of life may differ from another person's own, and it implies that your area of meditation may still vary with time.

Maybe you have a company that specializes primarily in the extraction of orange juice, and you are facing a challenge on how to preserve it. For sure you will meditate on how to preserve it, and that will be done at your leisure. Because it needs your total attention to figure out the complete measure to preserve your juice

The same is applicable to all other challenges that may occur in anything at all you are doing, just accept it and never waste time to think about it. You can meditate, and trust me there must be a way to sort the issue out. Even though the solution you discovered is such that you have to employ other people before it can work out, so be it. But the most important thing is that there's no problem without a solution, it can only take time. The reason why some of the things you see as a challenge may take time is because it's not time that it takes to solve weight loss issues that it will take to treat malaria sickness, as you know that malaria can be cured within a week range, but it may take months before a drug audit will fully recover, all because the process of drug audit recovery is a gradual process that needs time and patience, so you can't compare the two.

There are still individuals out there that can be trusted. Don't get me wrong if I said previously that you should not trust anyone, not trusting is part of life. But there are some situations where the only thing you will do to save yourself is to air your problem out to a certain individual who will listen to you and never in any form, betray you in the aspect you are seeking only the truth from them.

There are lots to talk about when it comes to acceptance power, but you can't overlook seeking support, as that is one of the means through which you can accept and have power.

Seeking support is very important. Maybe, as a couple, you got your wife pregnant. It doesn't mean that it's a problem, but if you are not a medical doctor, even if you are, I still suggest that you take out your time and look for a medical doctor who will bring out his time to pay attention during the duration of her pregnancy.

You will not necessarily be the one to look after her during that period. Meanwhile, when you seek someone to do that for you, you are seeking the person's support, and there's a level of trust you may have built with such a doctor in that the way he will handle your wife's issues may not be different from what you expected of him.

But mind you, any kind of support you are to seek from someone mustn't be the kind that will go beyond what is expected of that person. By this, I vividly want to remind you once again that it's very important to know when to say no and when yes is also important.

In hard circumstances, rely on friends, family, or a therapist for assistance. Speaking with reliable people about your emotions and experiences can bring comfort, understanding, and fresh insights.

Recognizing your emotions and treating yourself with kindness while you deal with the consequences of bad luck are the first steps toward acceptance. It's a slow process that entails accepting reality, developing resilience, and facing the future with bravery and compassion.

Chapter 3

Understanding the Limitations of "Why"

When incidents occur, the first thing that will come to one's mind is what was it that made this happen in this form, and when that happens automatically, you are already asking why. You heard that a friend of yours is celebrating, and what will come to your mind immediately is why he is celebrating. You will realize that he is either celebrating his birthday or something similar to that. If a friend of yours is celebrating and you ask why, it's really worth asking.

And that is to tell you why they are worth asking. There are some aspects where asking why can only limit us from moving ahead instead, what keeps revolving around our heads is the limitations in which the why we are asking keeps in our heads.

It's important to know when to ask why and when not to ask why. Instead of asking why, the only way forward is to move forward and embrace the situation with the lesson that accompanies it.

Which is the stepping stone to achieving greater success if the reason you asked why happened to be that you experienced unusual art or failure in your career? I do believe that it is not worth asking why.

When Thomas Alva Edison, who invented the electric bulb, was interviewed about how many times he failed and why he worked hard to invent the electric bulb, I marveled over what he said, but can we share this story together?

"How did it feel to fail 1,000 times?" was the question an interviewer asked.

In response, Edison said,

I did not fail a thousand times. The invention of the light bulb required 1,000 steps."

You may ask why for some reasons, but in the meantime, I will tell you that on your own, you may not have included how many steps it would take you to accomplish your aim in a particular project you are working on, and when you encounter thousands of failures in the process of trying to achieve that project, the only thing that will come to your mind is why am I experiencing this kind of failure?

You continue to think but look at the answer that Edison gave. I should ask you if you had in any way embarked on a project for which you experienced failure

You are left to answer the question by yourself, if he failed multiple times, instead of allowing the limitations of asking why to limit him from achieving his dream he moved on with a bold step and never looked at any one to set blame on.

you have to bear in mind that everything lies at the tips of your fingers, knowing fully well that when you call for celebration or when you achieve success in any area you are pursuing your dream, people may wish to listen to you to hear how you were able to achieve success, Probably if you include the number of times you failed before achieving success, they won't quarry you because they will definitely learn from both the success and unsuccessful story.

So, if you experience failure, why do you ask why? Asking why may come in different parenthesis. You may be asking why without knowing that you are already asking why, maybe I should explain better. My point is that you may open your mouth several times, asking yourself why, and you may also not open your mouth to do so, but when you allow yourself to be carried away by the incident that occurred you are already limiting yourself from moving forward.

What is in your mind at a particular point in time speaks a lot about your subconscious mind.

Have you ever experienced this kind of thing whereby you are writing something and suddenly someone by your side starts communicating with a person very close to you, and before you know it, you start including what the person is saying in your write-up?

Or am I the only person who has ever experienced such? That's an experience that I have witnessed for real. I had to call myself to others immediately after I discovered how crazy it was for me to join what someone was saying in my write-up.

That sounds funny, right? If you have had such an experience before, you will surely feel the same thing I felt when I witnessed it.

I use that to explain what your mind can feed to your sub-conscious mind if you have a challenge and you decide to keep your attention on the challenge instead of focusing on the lesson you are to learn from those challenges. When a problem occurs, it's either that the problem is such that you can learn a great lesson of life or that it's the one that will keep reminding you of the old memories, but whichever one you encounter, don't ask why rather, try to capture the great lesson that it came with and move on. It will definitely limit your ability to get positive results.

But that does not mean that you should be afraid of meeting challenges rather, prepare your mind at all times to accept things wholeheartedly without hurting yourself.

Understanding Anger and Its Limitations

How well do you act when it comes to anger management? Have you ever lost your temper and acted on it?

Well, people who are hurt-tempered can always attest to this. When you are acting on anger, there's every possibility that you may even pull a trigger on someone at that moment. The reason is that there is something behind your action at that moment that is not your fault, but basically, it's an action that you acted upon as a result of what you felt, which are usually your emotions.

When anger is not controlled, it can release devastating energies, much like a storm building inside a person. It starts as a tiny flame of resentment or unfairness, turning into a fire that swallows logic and perspective. We frequently find ourselves driven by its intensity in its flaming embrace, oblivious to the constraints it places on us.

Rage is essentially a primal reaction, an intense burst of energy activated by perceived threats or challenges. It is a normal aspect of being human and a warning sign that something is wrong that needs to be addressed. However, even the most alert minds might fall victim to traps hidden inside its ferocious grasp.

Anger's primary drawback is that it tends to impair judgment. In times of stress, impulses motivated solely by feelings take precedence over reason. Anger-fueled decisions frequently lack the insight and complexity necessary for practical problem-solving. In the heat of the moment, what seems reasonable may turn out to be regrettable later.

Anger also has the potential to escalate minor issues into larger disputes. Unchecked rage has the power to destroy relationships and sow discontent like a relentless river. Its destructive effects that affect mental and emotional health, as well as interpersonal relationships its corrosive effects also go inward.

Anger can also be a cunning companion, concealing underlying problems that need reflection and comprehension. It can act as a makeshift barrier, fending off hurt or weakness, but in the end, it blocks chances for development and recovery. Focusing just on the outward manifestation of anger might cause one to ignore the underlying currents of hurt, fear, or unfulfilled desires that feed its flames.

It's possible to resolve conflicts and express emotions in a better way when you acknowledge the limitations of rage. It asks us to hold off on making snap decisions and to take a moment to think things through. We may have more compassionately and clearly navigate the choppy waters of anger by practicing mindfulness and self-awareness.

A single strand among many makes up the human experience when it comes to rage. It is only through accepting its limitations and embracing its complexity that we may develop meaningful connections, empathy, and resilience. We find the way to real insight and transformation in this balance, in the middle of the emotional storm.

When we act on the flax of anger, there are things that we keep limiting ourselves from, and that is what we should be looking into right away.

Is anger manageable?

Can you control anger?

Truly, there are things that are considered manageable, and there are things that no one should think of managing.

Let assume that one acted upon anger and probably stabbed someone to death the person will be jailed as a result of what anger has caused him.

Thereby making him to find himself in a situation he wouldn't like to have much say over his life.

He won't be able to continue the pursuit of his dream and as well he has limited himself from some freedom of movement and also he has tagged himself a murderer which is already in his life history.

Then there are other minor things which it may have caused him in which he may be the only one who knows about it.

Why then do you allow yourself to get hurt and burn in anger beyond your control when you know that every problem has a solution and they are at the tips of your hands?

Can you on your own now access the level of your anger? Maybe by looking into some minor things you have done while you were burning on anger and letter discovered that you would have sorted it out if you had controlled it, remember that if there are tiny ones you have done without controlling your anger, mind you that when you may have repeated those tiny action severally it will automatically become a big habit in which you may need a very long period of time to recover from, and some day if you lose it totally on someone you may pull trigger on him there by limiting yourself from several freedom and causing more harm to your career .

But, in the aspect of anger management you are not alone on it, maybe you have find yourself severally in such mood in that you couldn't help issues other than to act on the influence of your anger I do believe that you need to follow a dual process on anger management because it's at the tips of hands to do that possibly if you dream of it like the normal way people dream of become great in life and work towards it and at the end they will achieve their dream too, you can achieve your dream of managing your anger and as well limit yourself from acting under the influence of anger.

Ways to control your anger is very important I may likely not go into detail, but I see that it will be very important if we look into it briefly.

RECOGNIZE TRIGGERS

"It's important to be mindful of your emotions before, during, and after experiencing a trigger. You might notice sudden feelings of sadness, discomfort, anxiety, or excitement. Physical reactions like chest pain or a strong emotional response may also occur. Understanding your reactions to triggers can help you recognize their presence.

Identifying triggers in your life is a personal journey that only you can undertake. Take the initiative to acknowledge what triggers you the most. Consider scheduling time during your leisure activities to reflect on these triggers, using pen and paper to document your thoughts.

It's time to address those triggering behaviors by regularly assessing and actively working to change them. If you find this process challenging, remember that you're not alone. We're in this together, and there's no need to feel apprehensive."

Reflecting on your experiences, you may have noticed that when a business deal falls through and causes a significant financial loss, it's natural to feel frustrated and express anger. However, it's important to recognize that such disappointments are part of business and shouldn't hinder your overall growth. Instead of reacting impulsively, it's valuable to extract lessons from these situations. Consider that the setback itself is a learning opportunity. Rather than immediately severing ties with the individual or service, take time to understand the underlying reasons for the failure. For instance, if you engaged an email writer who failed to deliver on time, explore whether there were external factors contributing to the delay. Perhaps the writer came highly recommended by a friend, or their past work appeared promising. By investigating these aspects, you can make informed decisions and avoid potential regrets.

Listen to him to understand what caused his disappointment. It could be due to illness and hospitalization for proper medical care. If this was why he couldn't meet you, you've realized it may not be his fault, and it's a matter that can be resolved promptly. Perhaps he excels at writing sales letters but fell ill unexpectedly. If the wait for his recovery doesn't align with your timeline, he may suggest someone else who can deliver the persuasive sales letters you need. The lesson here is that by rushing to replace him without understanding the situation, you risk ending up with someone who doesn't meet your requirements. Remember, the right person can elevate your business, and mishandling such situations can lead to chaos. This emphasizes the importance of managing anger and being aware of triggers to avoid self-harm and business setbacks.

Allocate time to address every challenge that arises you'll find that even a short amount of time can lead to positive outcomes in your favor.

Practice Relaxation Techniques

The question here is how do you express your anger? Are you the type that, whenever you are angry, you share tears, maybe the type that yells out, screaming out of your head, or the type that keeps silent, wondering why you burn like a flame inside you?

How much have you discovered about the means by which you express your anger?

Answer it on a piece of paper, and what is your answer like? Maybe I should tell you what I do whenever someone steps on my toes.

My wife refused to make a dinner for me. Maybe I was stressed out in my work place, I don't yell at her. I quickly work out of her after I might have heard from her the reason why she was unable to prepare a dinner. I go out there, take some glass of juice, and probably relax myself a little bit. I will take out time to see how I can handle such an issue whenever it occurs without acting on the influence of anger.

But before I go back home, I try to develop a repertoire of relaxation techniques such as deep breathing, meditation, or progressive muscle relaxation. These have always helped me and can also be of good help to you, as they can calm you down whenever your anger is rising.

You trusted someone, and the person back bit you. Does such an attitude still get you upset at all?

If so, know that disappointment has been there for ages and shouldn't be on the verge of pushing you to the wall.

TAKE A TIMEOUT

When anger starts to simmer, it's time to grasp the limitations of incessantly questioning "why" and opt for a timeout instead. This strategic pause involves stepping back from the heat of the moment, if feasible, and granting you a brief respite to cool off before tackling the issue head-on.

Anger has a cunning way of distorting our perceptions and propelling us towards impulsive reactions that often fuel rather than douse conflicts. By embracing the timeout approach, you carve out a space to recalibrate your perspective and approach the situation with renewed clarity.

During this interlude, focus on soothing the storm within. Whether through rhythmic breathing exercises, a brisk walk, or a few moments of silent introspection, redirect your attention away from the trigger of anger and towards a path of constructive engagement.

As tranquility settles, return to the fray with a tempered resolve. This enables you to articulate your emotions without the harsh edge of hostility, fostering a dialogue conducive to mutual understanding and resolution.

By acknowledging the limitations of constant "why" inquiries in moments of anger and opting for a timeout, you empower yourself to navigate conflicts with finesse, nurturing healthier connections along the way.

EXPRESS FEELINGS ASSERTIVELY

It involves communicating your thoughts, emotions, and needs in a clear, confident, and respectful manner. Here we are to go in depth on this skill, from its practical applications to its benefits.

Picture yourself confidently expressing your feelings, assured that your words hold significance and are received with respect and understanding. This is the essence of assertive expression, where you convey your emotions and thoughts with honesty and integrity without resorting to passive-aggressive behavior or bottling up your feelings.

One of the key benefits of expressing feelings assertively is the ability to build strong and genuine connections with others. When you communicate openly and honestly, you create a foundation of trust and mutual respect in your relationships. This can lead to deeper understanding, empathy, and a stronger sense of emotional intimacy.

In a professional setting, assertive communication can be a game-changer. It allows you to voice your opinions, ideas, and concerns effectively, leading to more productive discussions and collaborative outcomes. Assertive individuals are often seen as confident, reliable, and capable leaders who inspire trust and confidence in their teams.

Moreover, mastering the art of assertive expression can boost your self-esteem and self-confidence. When you speak up for yourself and assert your boundaries, you affirm your worth and value as a person. This confidence radiates in all aspects of your life, empowering you to tackle challenges, pursue your goals, and navigate difficult situations with grace and resilience.

However, it's essential to remember that assertive communication is not about being aggressive or confrontational. It's about finding the balance between expressing yourself authentically and respecting the feelings and perspectives of others. It requires active listening, empathy, and a willingness to engage in constructive dialogue.

It's a time of expressing feelings assertively, and you will discover a newfound sense of empowerment and authenticity. Your relationships will thrive, your professional endeavors will flourish, and most importantly, you will experience inner peace knowing that your voice matters and is heard.

USE POSITIVE SELF-TALK

It's important to know that when it comes to personal growth and mental well-being, the power of positive self-talk shines as a guiding light of resilience and inner strength. For navigating the complexities of life, mastering the art of monitoring your inner dialogue and shifting from negativity to positivity can be transformative. But before then, look into the potential and benefits of positive self-talk, exploring how it can empower you to cultivate a more optimistic and constructive mindset.

The potential of positive self-talk is vast and impactful. It serves as a powerful tool for self-awareness it allows you to recognize and challenge negative thought patterns. By becoming attuned to your inner dialogue, you can identify harmful beliefs and replace them with affirming and uplifting thoughts. This process not only fosters a sense of control over one's mindset but also cultivates a more positive mindset in the face of challenges.

Consider looking into it as a vital one, as the benefits of positive self-talk include the ability to enhance mental well-being. In the process of writing this book, I have done some research to engage individuals in positive self-talk experiences that reduce stress levels, improve mood, and increase overall psychological durability. By reframing negative thoughts into positive affirmations, you can build a strong foundation of self-confidence and self-esteem, leading to a more fulfilling and meaningful life.

In other words, positive self-talk encourage a growth mindset, encouraging you to embrace challenges as opportunities for learning and growth. Instead of viewing setbacks as failures, maybe you can adopt a more optimistic outlook, seeing setbacks as temporary hurdles on the path to success. This shift in perspective not only fuels motivation but also perseverance and determination in pursuing goals and dreams.

We are still learning about the significant benefits of positive self-talk and its impact on interpersonal relationships. When individuals cultivate a positive inner dialogue, they are more likely to exhibit empathy, kindness, and compassion towards others. This creates a positive ripple effect, fostering healthier and more fulfilling connections with family, friends, and colleagues.

In essence, the practice of positive self-talk empowers you to take full control of your mental and emotional well-being. It equips you with the tools to navigate life's challenges with optimism, and a growth mindset.

PRACTICE EMPATHY

Another effective way that will help you traverses the complex terrain of human emotions and viewpoints. If you are seeking to stimulate understanding and harmony in your interactions, practicing empathy is not just a skill but a transformative way of engaging with the world around us.

At its core, empathy is about stepping into someone else's shoes, not just figuratively but emotionally and cognitively. It's the ability to recognize and share the feelings of others, to see the world through your eyes, and to understand your unique experiences. This sagacious shift in perspective opens doors to deeper connections and meaningful communication.

I must tell you this because I see it as one of the remarkable potentials of empathy and its capacity to reduce hostility and conflict. When we take the time to truly listen to and empathize with others, we create a space for mutual respect and understanding to flourish.

Instead of approaching differences with defensiveness or aggression, empathy allows us to approach them with curiosity and openness. This shift in attitude can defuse tense situations and pave the way for constructive dialogue and collaborative problem-solving.

In other ways, practicing empathy offers a myriad of benefits, both personally and professionally. On a personal level, it cultivates compassion, emotional intelligence, and a sense of interconnectedness with others. It focuses on a sense of belonging and promotes healthier relationships built on trust, empathy, and mutual support.

We have to bear this in mind professionally empathy is a valuable skill in diverse fields such as leadership, counseling, customer service, and teamwork. You can now see that it's a valuable skill you can't do without. Empathetic leaders inspire trust and loyalty, creating inclusive and supportive work environments. In customer-facing roles, empathy enhances communication and enables service providers to meet the unique needs of individuals with care and understanding.

In essence, practicing empathy is not just a virtue but a practical approach to navigating the complexities of human interaction. It empowers you to bridge divides, build bridges, and forge meaningful connections that transcend differences.

Engage in Physical Activity

When we engage in physical activity, our bodies release endorphins, often referred to as "feel-good" hormones. These chemicals can uplift our mood, reduce stress, and create a sense of well-being. For someone struggling with guilt, these effects can be particularly knowledgeable. Physical activity offers a healthy outlet for pent-up emotions, allowing you to release tension and negative energy.

In other ways, regular physical activity can improve self-esteem and self-confidence. As you see improvements in your physical fitness and stamina, you often develop a more positive self-image. This shift in perception can be instrumental in overcoming feelings of guilt and self-blame.

Engaging in physical activities such as sports, yoga, or even regular walks outdoors can provide moments of mindfulness and relaxation. These activities allow you to focus on the present moment, letting go of past regrets and worries about the future. This mindfulness practice can contribute significantly to the healing process, nurturing a sense of acceptance and peace.

It's interesting to know that physical activity can serve as a distraction from rumination and negative thought patterns associated with guilt. By immersing oneself in an activity that requires concentration and effort, you can temporarily shift your focus away from self-critical thoughts, giving your mind a much-needed break.

You can cultivate the activities of blameworthiness healing, as it can be a gradual process without pushing yourself to extremes or seeking perfection in fitness goals. It's about finding enjoyable and sustainable ways to move the body, reconnect with oneself, and cultivate a positive mindset. Whether it's a brisk walk in nature, a calming yoga session, or a fun dance class, the key is consistency and finding activities that resonate with your preferences and needs.

USE HUMOR

When we find moments of laughter and joy amidst our struggles, it not only lightens our mood but also shifts our perspective, allowing us to see things from a different angle.

Humor has a unique way of breaking through the heavy clouds of guilt that weigh you down. It injects a dose of levity into your thoughts and emotions, reminding you that you are not defined by your mistakes or shortcomings. Instead, it encourages you to embrace your humanity, flaws and all, with a sense of self-compassion and acceptance.

Imagine a moment when you shared a hearty laugh with a friend or loved one. In that moment, the weight of bad conscience may have felt a little lighter as you allowed yourself to simply be in the present, enjoying the simple pleasure of laughter. This experience is not about denying the reality of your challenges but rather about finding moments of respite and connection that recharge your spirits.

Humor can also serve as a bridge between you and others, encouraging understanding and empathy. When we can laugh at ourselves or find humor in challenging situations, it opens the door to conversations that are lighthearted yet meaningful. It reminds us that we are not alone in our struggles and that there is shared humanity in our experiences.

SET BOUNDARIES

Setting boundaries is all about recognizing your own worth and deservingness of respect. It's about acknowledging that your feelings, opinions, and preferences are valid and worthy of consideration. This self-awareness forms the foundation for establishing boundaries that promote healthy relationships and self-care.

It's essential to be clear and specific about what is acceptable and what is not. This clarity helps prevent misunderstandings and allows others to understand your expectations. Communicating boundaries with empathy and understanding can lead to mutual respect and strengthen relationships.

Maybe it's for you to know how perplexing setting boundaries could be, especially when faced with resistance or pushback from others. It may require navigating uncomfortable conversations and standing firm in your decisions. This process of boundary-setting can be emotionally charged, but it is a necessary step towards reclaiming your autonomy and well-being.

In other ways, incorporating humor into the boundary-setting process is very important. Humor can lighten tense situations, ease communication barriers, and create a more positive atmosphere. It can be used to convey boundaries assertively yet tactfully, stimulating a sense of openness and understanding.

Should I say that setting boundaries is a skill that each and every one of us has to acquire because if you get it as a skill, you will practice self-awareness? It involves balancing assertiveness with empathy, respecting your own needs while considering the feelings of others. By mastering the art of setting boundaries, you empower yourself to create healthier relationships and cultivate inner peace.

And inner peace has a special test sweeter than honey, as honey test so sweet, so also does inner peace test our body and soul because you can't have peace of mind yet face emotional trauma.

So, don't you think that it's a skill worth acquiring?

Chapter 4

Releasing the Need for Explanations

There is an art that is above ordinary the art of letting go. It is a profound act, not of surrender but of liberation, where the shackles of incessant explanations are cast aside to embrace the uncharted realms of acceptance.

At the heart of this art lies a fundamental shift in perspective a shift from the relentless pursuit of answers to the gentle acceptance of what is. It is a journey that begins with understanding the futility of seeking exhaustive explanations for every twist and turn that life presents.

The essence of letting go is found in embracing uncertainty with open arms. It is in acknowledging that not everything needs a tidy explanation and that sometimes the beauty of life lies in its enigmatic nature. When we release the need for constant justification, we free ourselves from the burdensome weight of control.

Mindfulness becomes our ally in this journey. Through mindful awareness, we learn to observe our thoughts and emotions without judgment. We recognize that the incessant need for explanations often stems from a deep-seated desire for validation and approval. By cultivating self-compassion, we loosen the grip of self-doubt and pave the way for genuine acceptance.

By delineating our limits and honoring our needs, we create a space where explanations become unnecessary. We learn to say no without guilt and yes without reservation, navigating life with grace and authenticity.

The art of letting go is a master piece confirmation of buoyant, wisdom, and the deep beauty of surrender. It is a journey of paradoxes, where strength is found in vulnerability and liberation in release.

Understanding Acceptance

Looking at the concept of acceptance and its role in letting go of the need for explanations

Acceptance doesn't mean agreeing with everything that happens or condoning every action. Instead, it's about acknowledging the present moment without judgment or the burden of trying to change what cannot be changed. It's a radical act of self-compassion and empowerment.

We have to consider the insights into understanding acceptance.

Recognizing What You Can Control

You and I know that life itself is filled with uncertainties and challenges it's easy to feel overwhelmed and powerless. However, amidst the chaos lies a fundamental truth that can transform your life, recognizing what you can control. This simple yet intense concept is the key to unlocking personal empowerment and effectively managing stress.

At its core, understanding what you can control empowers you to take charge of your life. Instead of focusing on external factors or trying to change things beyond your influence, you shift your focus to what is within your reach. This shift in perspective is liberating, as it allows you to channel your energy and efforts into areas where you can make a real difference.

In other words, recognizing what you can control is powerful for managing stress. By acknowledging that not everything is within your control, you release yourself from the burden of trying to control the uncontrollable.

This acceptance brings a sense of calmness and flexibility, enabling you to navigate challenges with a clear mind and a steady heart.

Imagine waking up each day with a deep sense of empowerment, knowing that you have the ability to shape your destiny. Picture yourself facing adversity with confidence, understanding that while you may not control every outcome, you have the power to choose your response.

So, how can you start recognizing what you can control? Begin by identifying your sphere of influence the areas where your actions and decisions have a direct impact. Focus on honing your skills, setting realistic goals, and taking proactive steps towards your aspirations. Cultivate a mindset of adaptability and flexibility, embracing change as an opportunity for growth rather than a threat.

Remember, true strength comes from within. By recognizing what you can control, you unleash your potential, transform stress into strength, and improve on a journey of personal empowerment. It's time to take charge and embrace the power that lies in your hands.

Embracing Impermanence

Nothing in life remains static. Embracing impermanence revolves around the understanding that everything in life is transient, constantly changing, and impermanent. This includes our experiences, relationships, possessions, and even our own selves.

At its core, embracing impermanence involves cultivating a mindset that acknowledges and accepts the transient nature of life. It's about letting go of attachment to outcomes, expectations, and the illusion of control. Instead, it encourages us to live fully in the present moment, appreciating each experience and relationship for what they are without clinging to them excessively.

One aspect of embracing impermanence understands the impermanent nature of emotions and thoughts. We often get caught up in fleeting emotions, thinking they are permanent states. Embracing impermanence educates us to observe our emotions and thoughts without getting attached to them, knowing that they will come and go like passing clouds in the sky.

Furthermore, embracing impermanence can lead to a greater sense of freedom and liberation. When we let go of the need for things to stay the same or to last forever, we open ourselves up to new possibilities and experiences. We become more adaptable and resilient in the face of change, knowing that change is an inherent part of life.

Practically, embracing impermanence involves practices such as mindfulness and meditation. These practices help us cultivate awareness of the present moment, let go of attachments, and develop a deeper understanding of the impermanent nature of life.

Honoring Your Feelings

Honoring your feelings involves acknowledging the validity of your emotions, regardless of whether they are positive or negative. By honoring your feelings, you embrace your humanity and grant yourself permission to experience the full spectrum of emotions that make you who you are.

At times, it can be tempting to suppress or ignore certain feelings, especially those that are uncomfortable or painful. However, doing so only serves to bury these emotions deeper within, potentially leading to greater distress in the long run. Honoring your feelings means allowing yourself to feel and express them in a healthy and constructive manner.

When you honor your feelings, you also honor yourself. You recognize that your emotions are a natural response to your experiences, and they carry valuable insights about your needs, desires, and boundaries. By paying attention to your feelings, you gain valuable self-awareness and a deeper understanding of what truly matters to you.

Honoring your feelings strengthens your emotional resilience. Instead of bottling up emotions or pretending they don't exist, you confront them with courage and compassion. This empowers you to navigate life's challenges more effectively as you develop the ability to process and manage your emotions in a balanced way.

Cultivating Mindfulness

It's more important to observe thoughts objectively rather than to purge your minds. In your fast-paced lives, cultivating mindfulness can be a powerful means for finding peace amidst chaos.

Mindfulness on its own present to you essential key to learning and paying attention intentionally, being aware of your experiences, ideas, and emotions without allowing them to rule you is necessary for this.

It's like watching clouds pass by in the sky, acknowledging their presence but not clinging to them.

I wish to let you know that embracing mindfulness requires you to let go of the need to control everything. It's about surrendering to the flow of life and trusting that everything unfolds as it should. This doesn't mean being passive, but rather being proactive with a sense of inner calm.

Set yourself apart from others by knowing that mindfulness involves being compassionate towards ourselves and others. It's about treating ourselves with kindness and understanding, acknowledging that we are all human and imperfect. By practicing self-compassion, majorly you will cultivate a sense of inner peace.

You can't practice mindfulness without engaging fully well in each moment of your life. Whether you're eating, walking, or working, being present allows you to savor life's experiences more deeply. It's about bringing your full attention to whatever you're doing, enhancing your focus and productivity.

When it comes to your daily lives mindfulness doesn't require a huge time commitment. It can be as simple as taking a few deep breaths, pausing to notice your surroundings, or practicing gratitude for the present moment. These small acts of mindfulness can have a great impact on your overall well-being.

What lesson again would I have to live with you in the aspect life processes when it comes to cultivating mindfulness, you may encounter challenges and setbacks sure. It's important to approach these moments with curiosity and openness, viewing them as opportunities rather than obstacles. With perseverance and dedication, mindfulness can become a natural and empowering way of being.

Letting Go Of The Need For Explanations

Imagine a scenario where you find yourself constantly seeking explanations for every outcome or circumstance. This pattern can stem from a desire for control or a fear of uncertainty. However, the reality is that not everything in life comes with a clear explanation. Embracing this truth can be liberating, allowing you to navigate life with more ease.

Letting go of the need for explanations doesn't mean disregarding curiosity or critical thinking. Instead, it's about cultivating a mindset that is open to ambiguity and comfortable with not having all the answers. This shift in perspective can lead to greater inner peace and a deeper connection with the present moment.

Who do you explain to? To your inner self or to your closest friend, if it's about letting go of any situation trust me you don't need to explain to anyone rather move on and time will explain better.

Finding Meaning in Surrender

When talking about finding meaning in surrender, it is very, very important we look into it in these measure surrender isn't about giving up or losing control instead, it's an act of trust and acceptance.

See how we can focus on the measure of finding meaning in surrender.

Surrender As A Path To Liberation

Surrendering isn't a sign of failure in life but a gateway to finding inner freedom. It involves releasing the grip of resistance and embracing the flow of life. Through surrender, you let go of your illusion of control and open yourselves to the vast possibilities that unfold when you align with the natural rhythm of existence.

Embracing Uncertainty

Whenever you surrender, automatically you embrace uncertainty with courage and tenacity. It's recognition that life is inherently unpredictable, and your ability to find meaning lies in how you respond to the unknown. By letting go of rigid expectations and embracing the present moment, you will be entitled to discover a deeper sense of purpose and clarity.

Finding Strength In Vulnerability

You have to reconsider this fact that surrendering requires vulnerability, but also cultivates strength. It's in moments of surrender that you confront your fears and insecurities, allowing you to connect more authentically with yourselves and others. You have to know this as at when due that vulnerability becomes a source of Inner strength, fortitude growth and self-discovery.

Trust In The Process

Trust in yourselves in all circumstance, in the universe, and in the unfolding of life's mystery. It's a surrendering of the need to constantly control outcomes and instead, trusting that everything is happening as it should. This trust brings a sense of peace and alignment with your inner truth.

Transforming Challenges Into Opportunities

You may find it difficult to surrender, especially when you are having a hard time. However, it's in these moments of surrender that you will often experience the most important growth. By reframing challenges as opportunities for learning and transformation, you will empower yourselves to witness life's complexities with grace.

Embracing Surrender As A Practice

Ultimately, finding meaning in surrender is an ongoing practice a strategy of self-discovery and spiritual awakening. It's about embracing the paradox of letting go while remaining deeply rooted in your values and aspirations. Through surrender, you find not only meaning but also great liberation.

Chapter 5

Shifting Focus from why to what now

In our lives, challenges often confront us unexpectedly, leaving us puzzled and searching for answers. It's natural to ask ourselves, Why did this happen? Or what did I do wrong? These questions can lead to a spiral of confusion and self-doubt, hindering our progress and potential.

But what if we shifted our focus from dwelling on the why? To embracing what now? This shift in perspective is not just a change in words it's a better transformation of our mindset. Instead of getting stuck in the past or trying to dissect every detail of what went wrong, we can channel our energy into finding solutions and taking action in the present moment.

In the case of this question "why" to "what now" we assumed that it's a process of empowerment and self-discovery. It's about reclaiming control over your lives and embracing the opportunities that challenges bring. Rather than being defined by your setbacks, to make a good progress when challenges occur you must see every challenge as a stepping stones to growth.

By now I have to let you know that to shift in focus requires courage and a willingness to let go of the need for explanations. It's about trusting in your abilities and believing that you fully have what it takes to overcome obstacles. By adopting this mindset, you open yourselves up to new possibilities and pave the way for a brighter future.

So, the next time life throws a curveball our way, let's pause, and ask ourselves, "What now?" It's not about finding the perfect answer but about taking that first step forward with determination.

One of the most transformative shifts we can make is from asking "why" to ask "what now." When we fixate on the "why" of a situation, we often get entangled in unanswerable questions that drain our energy and stall our progress. However, when we shift our focus to "what now," we empower ourselves to take active steps forward. Instead of dwelling on the past or seeking explanations for every twist of fate, we direct our attention to the present moment and the opportunities it presents.

Empowering Acceptance Finding Peace In Uncertainty

Uncertainty is a constant companion. It lurks in the shadows of our aspirations, challenging us at every turn. Yet, within this uncertainty lies a moral opportunity for growth. It is in embracing acceptance that we find the key to unlocking peace amidst the anarchy.

Acceptance is not resignation it is the courageous acknowledgment of reality as it is I have to repeat myself again. It is a declaration of your willingness to engage with life on its terms, rather than futilely resisting what we cannot change. When we embrace acceptance, we free ourselves from the burdens of denial and resistance, allowing us to channel our energy towards constructive action.

Finding peace in uncertainty is not about eliminating all doubts or uncertainties. Instead, it is about cultivating a mindset that thrives in the midst of equivocal. It is the ability to hold space for uncertainty without letting it consume us. This requires a delicate balance of surrender and willingness to surrender control over the uncontrollable while staying salient in the face of challenges.

Moving Forward Without Answer no

The quest for answers can indeed consume a significant amount of time and energy. It's natural to seek clarity and understanding, especially when faced with uncertainty or challenges. However, what if the true essence of growth isn't found solely in having all the answers? What if, instead, it lies in the courageous act of embracing the unknown?

Embracing the unknown with courage is a transformative mindset. It's about shifting focus from the relentless pursuit of answers to the acceptance of pandemonium and the possibilities it holds. When we embrace the unknown, we open ourselves up to new experiences, opportunities, and insights that may not have been visible within the confines of certainty.

Courage plays a vital role in this process. It takes courage to step into the unknown, to face uncertainty without succumbing to fear or doubt. It's about acknowledging that growth often occurs outside our comfort zones, in the uncharted territories of life where answers may be scarce but discoveries abound.

By embracing the unknown with courage, we free ourselves from the shackles of perfectionism and the pressure to have it all figured out. We become more adaptable, resilient, and open to learning from every experience, whether it brings clarity or confusion.

Understanding The Nature Of Uncertainty

Uncertainty is not a barrier but a bridge to new possibilities. It challenges us to step outside our comfort zones and explore uncharted territories. By accepting that not every challenge comes with a predefined solution, we open ourselves to a world of learning and personal growth.

The Myth Of Certainty

Society often portrays certainty as the ultimate goal, associating it with success and fulfillment. However, the relentless pursuit of certainty can lead to anxiety and frustration when faced with life's complexities. True empowerment comes from embracing uncertainty as a natural part of the human experience.

Thriving in Uncertainty

Moving forward without all the answers do not mean wandering aimlessly. It involves cultivating a mindset of adaptability, learning to navigate challenges with grace and confidence. By embracing uncertainty, as at your early 20s you can discover the inner strength and unlock your full potential.

CHAPTER 6

Escaping The Why Trap

Reasoning is grounded in what we know to be true. However, our knowledge is inherently limited because it's confined to what we've experienced or learned. We can reason about what we know and even what we know we don't know. But does this cover everything we could possibly know?

Surely not. Maybe I have to take it to a ground level have you ever witnessed a young child drawing a seemingly absurd conclusion? They base their reasoning on what they know and what they understand they don't know, sometimes leading to comical outcomes from an adult perspective. Yet, their logic is sound from their own perspective.

Consider this example, when my daughter was very young, my wife and I prioritized feeding her healthy foods, often in green, yellow, or orange hues. One day, my wife handed our daughter a strawberry. She was thrilled but treated it like a toy, not food, because in her world, food was never red.

You might think this is typical behavior for kids, but wait until you hear about the chocolate ice cream incident.

Our kid was excited to taste chocolate ice cream when my wife first offered it to her. But every time my wife tried to feed her, she didn't succeed. This small child loved to eat, but she grew more and more irritated since, to her, brown, wet, mushy objects weren't supposed to be eaten. She wasn't persuaded because she had experienced textures like these previously. Her mother was reluctant at first, but eventually her enthusiasm for chocolate ice cream triumphed over her doubts.

How To Escape The Trap Why

Imagine yourself perched on the brink of an impractical reality. How do you cross this line without losing the knowledge gained by reason and the rewards of your laborious experiences? The key is too momentarily, if only momentarily, suspend reason a modest but powerful act. There is so much possibility for change at that very instant. Let rid of your cynicism and consider what mysteries exist in the world outside the limits of reason?

You might not have realized how important it is to get out of the trap on your own. However, you should think about asking yourself these questions and considering the replies.

If probably the answer I hinted at is not as good as your own perspective, you are still advised to give a suitable answer to those questions.

Question: How do you navigate the boundary between reason and a reality beyond it without losing the wisdom gained through rationality?

Answer: One way is by temporarily suspending reason, even if just for a moment. This act allows you to explore new perspectives and possibilities while retaining the valuable truth acquired through rational thinking.

Question: What benefits can be gained from momentarily setting aside disbelief and considering the world beyond reason?

Answer: By doing so, you open yourself up to new ideas, perspectives and potential solutions that may not be accessible within the confines of strict rationality. This can lead to greater creativity, understanding, and personal growth.

Finding Strength In Ambiguity

True progress frequently occurs outside our comfort zones, which is leadership training programs frequently address this idea.

I just came into an instance that really put my ability to tolerate uncertainty to the test. It was a good lesson in accepting uncertainty in addition to being an amazing event. My inner doubts were echoed by questions like "Where is the water?" and "Are there snakes here?" Every new obstacle served as a "past-frail" reminder that overcoming discomfort may fortify and fortify us as leaders rather than a pass-fail exam.

New events in life might or might not live up to our expectations. Nonetheless, they are priceless chances for development, teaching us that effective leadership and personal progress depend on our ability to manage suffering.

The journey outlined within these pages is not about finding a definitive path to certainty. Instead, it is a gentle nudge towards self-discovery and toughness, reminding us that true trust and empowerment stem from within.

As we reflect on the themes of releasing the need for constant justification and reframing challenges as opportunities for growth, we are encouraged to shift our focus from dwelling on the "whys" of the past to embracing the "what now" of the present moment. This shift in perspective focuses on a sense of flexibility and adaptability, essential qualities for traverse lives convolute and turns.

Question on Your Head sheds light on the nuanced dynamics of human relationships, cautioning against placing undue trust only based on past achievements. It emphasizes the importance of discernment and integrity, guiding readers towards a deeper understanding of character and authenticity.

Within these stories of triumph over doubt and flexibility in uncertainty, we find the transformative power that encourages and redefine our own journeys. As we turn the final page of this book, may we carry with us the lessons learned and embark on our paths with renewed clarity, conviction, and a steadfast focus on the possibilities that lie ahead.